Human Interests

STANFORD SERIES IN PHILOSOPHY

Editorial Board

HUMAN INTERESTS
Reflections on
Philosophical Anthropology

Nicholas Rescher

Stanford University Press, Stanford, California   1990

Stanford University Press, Stanford, California
© 1990 by the Board of Trustees of the Leland Stanford Junior University
Printed in the United States of America

CIP data appear at the end of the book

FOR MY CHILDREN

Preface

THE ESSAYS presented here were mostly written during 1987–88, largely under the inspiration of a reading of Miguel de Unamuno's 1913 classic, *Del sentimiento trágico de la vida* (finally in the original—for even an old dog can learn new tricks). As a disciple of Leibniz, I am inclined to a more optimistic view of the human condition than this great but somber Spanish thinker. Still, the contemplation of his ideas offered me the welcome occasion to give written expression to some of these variant appreciations.

In writing the book, I have profited from comments on draft versions by David Carey and Madeline Larson. And I am grateful to Marian Kowatch for preparing a workable typescript through the course of numerous revisions. Some of the discussions presented here lean substantially on prior publications—in particular chapters 5, 12, 13, and 16. Detailed acknowledgments are made in the footnotes.

N.R.

Contents

Human Interests

Introduction: Philosophical Anthropology

PHILOSOPHY is a many-roomed mansion. It includes the philosophy of nature, the philosophy of law, the philosophy of science, the philosophy of art—the philosophy of this, and the philosophy of that. But one of its most important departments is philosophical anthropology, the philosophical study of the conditions of human existence and the issues that confront people in the conduct of their everyday lives.

The theoreticians of Greek antiquity took philosophy to center around just this issue of intelligent living—of determining the nature of a life lived under the guidance of reason, our characteristic endowment as *Homo sapiens*. Such a perspective puts philosophical anthropology at the top of the philosophical agenda—a position it contested with the philosophy of nature throughout classical antiquity. In more recent times, however, its prominence has declined—no doubt because modern man's achievements have been more notable in the natural than in the human sciences.

Philosophical anthropology is a fundamentally normative discipline whose mission is to study what is involved in "the good life." It examines the human condition with a view to identifying the modes of thought and action that enable people to take rational satisfaction in what they are doing with their lives. When Oliver Cromwell said that what matters for people is "not what they want, but what's good for them," he spoke like a philosophical anthropologist. The prime aim of the subject is to identify and clarify the things that people should give attention to because to neglect them impoverishes their lives. Its concern is with the matters that people should—and, if sensible, would—seek to employ as governing principles in the management of their lives. Accordingly, philosophical anthropology treats primarily the value aspect of human existence, inquiring into what is of particular interest to us and what is of particular importance for us. (These are not necessarily the same; the maintenance of our health is important but generally not very interesting; the history of our own ancestors is interesting but generally not very important.)

The topics of philosophical anthropology are first and foremost the items indicated by the format of an identity card: individuality (via a *name*), *age, sex, nationality, religion*, and work (*profession*). These are the salient things that provide us with the most crucial pieces of information we need and want to have regarding the people with whom we have to deal. And they are factors that profoundly affect each of us as we confront the daily business of getting on with our own lives.

Philosophical anthropology thus deals preeminently with *conditio humana*, with the matters that are properly of concern to people at large and in general. It does not address matters of particular, person-differential concern—special interests or talents that one individual may have and another lack. What matters for the philosophical anthropologist is that all people everywhere have an interest in finding a mode of work—of quotidian endeavor—that they can regard as worthwhile and rewarding. But whether they are to be butchers or bakers or candlestick makers is no longer of relevance. The horizons of the subject are universal. Accordingly, the task of philosophical anthropology is *not* to articulate a personal philosophy of life—a set of rules and practical precepts that a particular individual finds helpful in the pursuit of his or her personal goals. It does not deal with one's idiosyncratic views, preferences, reliefs, predilections. Rather, it seeks to examine and clarify the general aspects of the human condition that hold good for everybody, addressing the issues that any sensible person should confront because they represent matters of importance and concern for people at large. The business of philosophical anthropology is thus with the universal principles that should lie at the basis of one's own particu-

lar approach to life. (Think of the medical analogy: "Eat health-
fully" applies to everyone, "Avoid sugar" only to some.)

It is clear on this basis that philosophical anthropology is not
the philosophy *of* anthropology. It does not address (as, say, the
philosophy of physics does) the question of the methodology of
a certain scientific discipline and the interpretation of its findings. Anthropology as such is an empirical, descriptive discipline that inquires into how people actually live in various conditions and circumstances. Philosophical anthropology, on the
other hand, is concerned with evaluative deliberations about the
good life—with ideals and with normative questions about how
people ought ideally to live. (Philosophical anthropology bears
somewhat the same relation to empirical anthropology/sociol-
ogy that utopian social philosophy bears to political science.)

The founding father of philosophical anthropology as an
independent discipline was Immanuel Kant (b. 1724). In his
Anthropologie in pragmatischer Hinsicht (1789), he distinguished
between "*scientific*" anthropology (*physiologische Anthropologie*),
which undertakes an empirical investigation of man's life in the
world of nature, and "*pragmatic*" anthropology (*pragmatische Anthropologie*), which investigates man as a free agent who can and
does shape himself through his own free actions in a way that
admits and indeed demands rational investigation. Various of
Kant's immediate followers (such as Jacob Friedrich Fries, b.
1773, and C. F. Burdock, b. 1776) gave new impetus to philosophical anthropology as a special discipline of its own, and it
gradually established itself as such among the philosophers of
Germany, where it flourished particularly in the period between
the two world wars, Max Scheler being perhaps its principal
exponent.[1]

The second half of the twentieth century has seen a decided
neglect of philosophical anthropology, particularly in the Anglo-
American orbit. The rampant relativism of the age has apparently made philosophers feel uncomfortable about discussing
the things that people would be well advised to do with their
lives. A pervasive ethos of "judge not" and "live and let live"

---

[1] See particularly his *Die Stellung des Menschen im Kosmos* (Darmstadt, 1928).
For an informative sketch of philosophical anthropology on historical principles,
see Bernard Groethuysen, *Philosophische Anthropologie* (Munich, 1928).

has left philosophers feeling hesitant to offer normative judgments about the positive human good—as contrasted with a negative condemnation of patently malign practices like genocide or racism. But though such an attitude may well be understandable, it is not justifiable. Even as war is too important to be left to the generals, so philosophizing is too important to be left to journalists.

Yet how can the conclusions of such a normative enterprise be validated? Is it not all just a matter of pontificating about one's own evaluative sentiments? By no means! Such subjectivism can be transcended by testing one's value judgments against the experience of others—and in particular the experience of those who manage to find real satisfaction in living a life based on basic principles that elicit a fair degree of general approval. For in evaluating, as in inquiring, what counts most in the final analysis is the test of experience—of experimentation in the old sense that this term still carries in Spanish (unlike French or English).

The subject is large, but this book is small. The essays it collects together do not constitute a comprehensive "system" of philosophical anthropology. Rather, they represent a series of explorations, of forays into various important sectors of the subject that are closely connected with other philosophical issues—particularly in the areas of epistemology and ethics. Though the topics treated largely reflect my own interests, there is nevertheless some rhyme and reason to their selection, since they generally represent either *mandatory* topics that must be treated in this field or *neglected* topics to which the literature of the field has not given just due.

The methods of the book are largely "analytical"—concerned to probe into the details of issues, not to provide a large "synthetical" systematization. But even this more modest endeavor has its utility. In helping to clarify the issues, it puts into sharper focus the choices that confront us in the management of life's affairs. Here, as elsewhere, analysis may not resolve these choices, but it nevertheless facilitates their management through sensible reflection.

A constant leitmotiv of these essays is the ambiguous position of reason on the guidance of human affairs. On the one hand, reason is of our very nature, and our commitment to it is absolute. On the other hand, we cannot avoid recognizing that life being what it is, the counsel of reason—though the best we have—is nonetheless imperfect. Human life is too chaotic and chancy for reason to prove as effective a guide as its devotees would ideally like.

Philosophical anthropology deserves our attention precisely because we *are* human beings and should, in consequence, be concerned for those things that are specifically human. The question of the sorts of things we should do with our opportunities in this world—of how we should spend that rarest and least renewable resource of all, our life itself—is undeniably a key issue for us. Now, as always, it behooves people to think reflectively about the ways and conditions of living that make for a rewarding life for themselves and their fellows. The question of how we should manage our lives so as to realize for ourselves, our fellows, and our posterity the positive values that life's opportunities afford us is clearly one of the most crucial issues for philosophers and indeed for people at large. The deliberations of philosophical anthropology are every bit as important and useful now as they were at the dawning of the subject in classical antiquity.

What Is a Person?

PERHAPS the most significant and far-reaching single fact about us is that we are *persons*. For it is this, above all, that determines our self-image and our self-understanding—our views of the sort of beings that we ourselves are. Our being persons (duly self-appreciative rational agents) is even more important for us—more crucial to our status in the world's scheme of things—than our being people (members of the species *Homo sapiens*).

But what is it to be a person? Seven conditions are essential:

1. *Intelligence*. One must be an intelligent being, able to acquire and process information—to acquire, maintain, and modify consciously held beliefs about the world and one's place within it.

2. *Affectivity*. One must be able to evaluate, to react to developments in the affective range of positive/negative, seeing the world's developments as good or bad, fortunate or unfortunate. A being that lacks preference, that views everything with indifference (threats to its own very existence included) would not be a person.

3. *Agency*. One must be capable of goal-oriented action as a *free agent* who is able not only to *pursue* goals, but to *initiate* them, to set them for oneself. As philosophers have insisted since Aristotle's day, persons are not merely agents, but *autonomous* agents whose goals proceed from within their own thought

processes and who are accordingly responsible for their acts.[1]

4. *Rationality.* One's actions (including mental actions like beliefs and evaluations) must proceed under the aegis of intelligence. They must by and large proceed from *reasons* that are grounded in aims and values to which one is committed.

5. *Self-understanding.* One must *understand* oneself in these terms, that is, conceive of oneself as an intelligent free agent, operating in the dimension of belief, action, and evaluation.

6. *Self-esteem.* One must *value* oneself on this basis and see this aspect of oneself as an important and valuable feature. That is, one must have a self-respect rooted in one's appreciation of oneself as an intelligent free agent.

7. *Mutual recognizance.* One must be disposed to acknowledge other duly qualified agents as persons and be prepared to value them as such. With persons there must be not only feeling, but fellow-feeling; persons must function in a context of community.

These conditions are severally necessary and jointly sufficient conditions for qualifying as being "a person" in the standard sense of the term. A person is thus a being who can function in certain characteristic ways and goes about doing certain sorts of things—who operates in the sphere of ideation, evaluation, and action. The concept of a "person" is accordingly a complex one that involves many constituent components—both descriptive and normative. However, one cannot be more or less of a person. Being a person turns simply on whether or not certain specific requirements are met. Personhood is a matter of yes or no, not one of degrees: a given creature either is or is not a person.

Note that conditions (1)–(4) relate to what a person *can* do (viz., think, evaluate, act, reason), while conditions (5)–(7) relate to what a person *does* do, to the sort of use that is made of those abilities. To be a person one must use one's capacities in a certain sort of way (in point of self-understanding, self-esteem, and mutual recognizance). And this means that those who deem themselves to be persons—who "stake a claim" to be such—

---

[1] Note that *agency* itself has various further ramifications. For example, agents must have a time dimension—of a future with reference to which they plan and a past for whose actions they can be responsible.

must in consequence assume from sheer self-consistency an obligation to endeavor to comport themselves in this way. Accordingly, the idea of a person has an indelibly moral dimension.

It is emphatically not enough to be an intelligent agent to be a person. Otherwise the higher primates would be persons. To be a person, one must not only be conscious, but be self-conscious: one must not only be a *knower* of facts and a *performer* of action, but be *aware of oneself* as such—one must think of oneself as such. A person must not only possess knowledge, but possess knowledge of a very special sort, namely, self-knowledge. In view of this fact, even the possession of reason does not suffice to make a person. (Boethius's definition of a person as a rational being, "persona est naturae rationalis individua substantia," simply will not do.[2]) A merely rational being can be less than a person.

Still, rationality—the feature of having most of what one does proceed from the motivation of reasons—is a salient characteristic of personhood. And this rationality pertains to belief, evaluation, and action alike. Accordingly, persons are not just *affective* but also *evaluative* creatures. Their reactions pro and con do not proceed on the basis of feelings alone—of pleasures and pains, likes and dislikes. They involve approval and disapproval, evaluations that are based on reasons. The preferences of sensible persons in matters of thought, action, and evaluation generally can be and frequently are assessments—evaluations based on reasons. As rational beings, persons must be able to "give an account of themselves"—to render what they do in matters of belief, action, and evaluation intelligible (to themselves of course, but thereby also potentially to others).

Persons are free and responsible agents. They are free and responsible in that when they act they "*could* have acted otherwise" in the specific sense that they *would* have acted otherwise if the circumstances had been different. (The explanatory unraveling of this "if" clause is a very long story, for whose telling the present occasion is not the most suitable.) Accordingly, personhood involves autonomy and self-direction. It means that a full and adequate explanation of what an agent *does*, (in contrast to "what happens to" him or her) requires reference to what this

[2] *Du duabus naturis*, cap. 3.

agent is and wants, values, prefers, or the like. Free agents are beings for whom conscious wants and preferences—rather than mere instincts and urges alone—provide determinants of action.

To be a person, one must be able to act freely—one must have "free will." Does this mean that there would cease to be any persons if it turned out that the world is wholly a theater of materialistic/deterministic causal processes? Not necessarily. For if there were an "inner determinism"—if an agent's actions were the causal product of the operation of its own materialistic brain—then the causal condition of effective control over one's own actions would still be satisfied. The freedom at issue is not freedom from any and all determination, but freedom from *external* control—which is compatible with an internally rooted determinism via an agent's own motives and "states of mind." The crux of the moral autonomy at issue in personhood is that an adequate understanding of the agent's actions requires making a reference to lives or their thought processes.

Accepting people as rational free agents who bear the moral responsibility for their actions is an integral part of seeing someone as a person. It is not that we have somehow *learned* this; rather, it reflects an indefeasible presumption (analogous to the presumption that a minor is incapable of rape or murder). The generalization that "persons are rational free agents" is a tautology. The particularization "X is a person" is the product not of an *inference*, but of a decision—"I shall treat X as a person"—a decision that should be authorized by the observational evidence but cannot be totally constrained by it. In recognizing someone as a person, as an autonomous, free, responsible, rational agent, we do not passively reflect observed facts about them, but are actively engaged in treating them in a certain sort of way—failing which we would fall not so much into *epistemic* as into *moral* error.

Personhood stands at one end of a complex spectrum. Each of us forms the center of a many-circled social world. Around us there proliferate innumerable social units and groups to which we belong, be it by choice or by the hand of fate: families, clans, fellow employees, team- or club-mates, fellow citizens or countrymen, coreligionists, members of our cultural group in our civilization, the human race, and, last but not least, the wider, potentially cosmic confraternity of rational beings at large. We are by nature placed within a large, variegated series of overlapping and complexly intersecting groupings. Each carries certain commitments, obligations, and duties, from the smallest unit or member of a particular family to the very largest—the community of persons, of rational agents at large.

Interestingly, it does not lie in the concept of a person that one must have a body. To be sure, one must be able to act, but this agency could in theory be purely mental—involving solely, say, the communication between minds. Only contingently—only in worlds (such, presumably, as ours) where the transmission of information requires sending physical signals—will persons have to be embodied.

Becoming a Person

To be a person one must think of oneself in a certain sort of way. One must view oneself as a *self*, an intelligent free agent with a unified identity over time whose present decisions reflect a responsibility for past action and whose present commitments are to be taken as binding for the future.

Persons accordingly are constituted by self-definition. It is how we see ourselves, both as individuals and in relation to others, that makes us what we are. Being a person calls for thinking of oneself in a certain sort of way—as an intelligent free agent who, by virtue of this circumstance, is a possessor of worth and a bearer of rights in relation to others. In this regard, then, to see oneself in a certain sort of way (viz., as a person) is through this very act to make a certain sort of thing of oneself (a person). In this sense, persons are "self-made": being a person is a matter of having a certain sort of self-image. It requires conceiving of ourselves as a person—as an intelligent free agent who is capable of acting in line with our own choices and conducting our interactions with others on a basis of reciprocity. Accordingly, to be a person one must have the conception of a person—or a pretty close approximation thereto.

Persons are evaluative beings. Not only must they be able to *believe* and to *act* in the light of their beliefs, but their actions must be geared to values: to preferences and priorities on whose basis a rational being can see the objects of its desires as being desirable. Evaluation is crucial to personhood. And this matter of evaluation is pervasive. In particular, persons can evaluate their values—can endeavor to assess the extent to which they are rationally defensible.

Miguel de Unamuno asked, "If we are in this world *for* some purpose, whence could this 'for' be taken but from the very depths of our will?"[3] But this oversimplifies the matter. Our purpose, our "mission in life," is not elective but inheres in what we *are*—it lies not in our *will* but in our *nature*. Its roots lie not in what we want but in what we are—or in what we find ourselves to be in the course of our efforts at self-understanding. To be a person is to be a creature that thinks of itself as having a mission—a commitment to realize in and for itself the values that are at issue in being a person.

To *be* a person one must accordingly have the *concept* of a person. This is why, at bottom, other higher primates—or, for that matter, our hominid ancestors—do not qualify as persons. Such creatures can all think and choose and act. But presumably their conceptual repertoire is too impoverished to enable them to think of themselves as such, that is, as beings who can think and choose and act in the light of those choices. To be a person requires having a certain sort of self-image, and early on in the history of our race the reflexive conception of a self was presumably missing or underdeveloped. Until people developed the rather sophisticated conception of "personal selves" as "intelligent free agents" they were not persons. To be a person one must deem oneself as such; and this involves thinking of oneself as a certain kind of being, an agent who acts and (at least potentially) *interacts* with others of its own kind, a being who takes causal and moral responsibility for its own actions.

A person is accordingly a complex sort of being. In consequence of this circumstance, very different conceptions of personhood are in circulation. On the one side lies the Hegelian approach, which conceives personhood in terms of one's position in relation to others within the framework of a social order. The crux of personhood lies in the mutual recognizance and reciprocal acceptance that characterizes one's acceptance by others. On the other side lies the Nietzschean approach, which conceives of

---

[3] "Si estamos en el mundo *para* algo, de dónde puede sacarse ese *para* sino del fondo mismo de nuestra volundad?" Miguel de Unamuno, *Del sentimiento trágico de la vida*, ed. P. Felix Garcia (Madrid, 1982), p. 226.

persons as entirely self-made. For Nietzsche, a personal self is something one becomes through asserting one's independence of all else and insisting on the privacy of one's own inwardness. One forms oneself as an authentic person by asserting a scale of self-oriented values as guides for fashioning a life of one's own—even as an artist creates his work by imposing his inner demands on the materials at hand. But the fact is that both of these approaches are one-sided and imbalanced. Personhood is a holistic complex that embraces both elements. A person without idiosyncrasies—without the evaluative basis for an inwardly imposed stance toward the outer world—is a mere empty shell. But someone who exists only unto himself, without relationships of community and interrelationships with others, is enmeshed in a delusional detachment from the world's course of things that makes him a freak rather than a person. The self-assertion of personhood and its coordinate, self-understanding, are both modes of relating oneself to others, and the reciprocal recognizance of persons is a matter of appreciating and valuing the fact that we all have the right and the duty to an inner life of our own, providing for various strictly personal aims and values. Personhood combines two sides, the one directed inward, the other outward. To assert the predominance of one to the exclusion of the other is to stunt and distort the conception at issue.

The Value Dimension

Personhood is something inherently normative. To be a person in the full sense of the term is to see oneself as capable of acting in the light of values appropriately deemed valid. Specifically, this means that one must value personhood itself. As long as personhood is not valued for what it is, the conception of it still remains unachieved. But if I am to see myself as rationally entitled to consideration because I have a certain status X (because I am a person), then I must see X as a generally consideration-underwriting feature: if it entitles *me* to consideration, it correspondingly entitles *anybody*. Thus if I expect consideration—let alone respect—from others because I have X, then I must myself be prepared to respect X in others. The principles of rational cogency are impersonal: they do not respect the peculiarity of individuals. One's self-perception as a person must be such as to lead one to require certain claims and entitlements to consideration, to having one's own claims and needs taken into account. (From early childhood on the idea of getting and giving one's due—of "playing fair"—comes into it.)

To be a person is thus to see oneself (and other persons) as units of worth and bearers of rights. A full-fledged conception of personhood can develop only in a social context. To regard oneself as a possessor of worth and a bearer of rights *in virtue of being a person* is thereby to accord a certain status to persons in general. It is to see persons in general as occupying a special place in the scheme of things—as constituting a special category of beings with whom one has a particular kinship and toward whom one consequently bears particular responsibilities.

Accordingly, the evaluative dimension is crucial to the full-fledged conception of a person. To have this conception of oneself is not only to consider oneself a being of a certain kind but to *value* oneself for it—that is, to deem oneself a bearer of value for this very reason. And this requires generality. We cannot sensibly value personhood in ourselves except by valuing personhood as such, and consequently valuing it also in others. (For example, a being entirely unmoved by the suffering of others of its own kind would not qualify as a person.)

The Communal Aspect

We are born *people* (members of the species *Homo sapiens*), but become *persons*. Only as we progress through childhood and learn to think of ourselves as responsible agents—intelligent free individuals interacting with others as such—do we become persons. (No doubt this communal development reflects a tendency that evolutionary processes have programmed into our developmental history, so that personhood is de facto more closely affixed to humanity than abstract theory alone suggests.) Personhood does not represent a biological mode of existence within organic nature, but a social mode of existence within an environing culture. Personhood thus has an inextricably social dimension. The conception of a (full-fledged) person is subject to a principle of reciprocity-expectation. For to qualify as a person oneself involves acknowledging and accepting as such the other creatures who seem plausibly qualified as being persons. And it involves the expectation that they will reciprocate. In deeming others as persons, and thereby as entitled to being valued as such—qualified to have me treat *their* interests, their rights and concerns, as deserving of *my* respect—I expect them to see me in exactly this same light. Consequently, if others whom I recognize as persons treat me as a mere thing, and not as a person, it injures my own personhood; it undermines my ability to see myself as a person.

William James says that we will be moral beings only if we believe that we are free agents, because only then will we deliberate about our actions with a view to reasons and thereby become morally responsible for them. But the real point here is a more fundamental one. It is precisely because persons as such form part of a mutually recognizant community of rational agents that persons are ipso facto beings who fall within the domain of morality. Morality does not inherently root in a social compact. If extraneous persons were to come upon the scene—perhaps from outer space—we would at once have certain moral obligations to one another (to respect one another's "rights" as persons and the like), which would certainly not need to be products of a prior agreement, real or tacit.

To be a person is to have a certain sort of self-image. But what of small children, the mentally handicapped, the merely heedless or thoughtless, and so on. What are we to say of someone who, for one reason or another, never forms any real self-image at all? Should we say that they thereby disqualify themselves as persons?

Well . . . yes and no. On the one hand, they do not, strictly and literally, satisfy the standards of personhood. But this does not quite settle the matter. For to be a person is not only to make certain *claims* for oneself but also to make corresponding *concessions* to others. In particular, it involves giving others the benefit of doubt when it comes to acknowledging them as congeners, as fellow persons. Accepting *them* as qualified persons is implicit in *our* claims to personhood. The class of authentic persons—of people who see themselves as such—constitutes a family united by a bond of mutual respect. Part and parcel of what defined one as a person is the "professional courtesy" (as it were) of acknowledging others as such—the preparedness to accept them as members of "one larger family" that includes oneself and one's more immediate associates.

Moreover, the limits of this family do not stop at the boundaries of the human community. If there are other, nonhuman rational agents in the universe whom we have good reason to see as possessed of a sufficiently developed self-image to value themselves as such, then we would have to accept them as persons also.

But what can one say about those who dilate the boundaries of personhood, who propose to exclude women, say, or children, or strangers from this domain? Simply that they thereby put their own personhood in doubt. For being a person requires having the concept of a person, and those whose conception is flawed in this way thereby compromise their claims to having an adequate grasp of the concept. It is part and parcel of the value dimension of personhood to acknowledge and esteem as a fellow person those who (like the very young) have the potential for a future exercise of the capacities of personhood (intelligent agency, etc.) and also those who (like the incapacitated old) have the dignity of a previously manifested exercise of these capacities. Those who do not recognize and value other plausible person-candidates as such thereby cast their own personhood into doubt.

There is, of course, a domain of artificial *intelligence* that is nowadays much in the air—and in the news. But is there also a domain of artificial *personhood*? When—or rather if—we are led to acknowledge that computers can "think," must we then also acknowledge them as persons? Clearly not!

As we saw at the outset, among the essential elements of personhood are (1) intelligence, (2) rational agency, (3) self-assertion, and (4) social reciprocity. With computers, (1) seems possible and perhaps even plausible. But (2) is problematic, and (3) and (4) are out of reach. Or that at least is how the matter looks at present. Were the situation ever to change so radically that good reason exists for granting that "thinking machines" can achieve capacities (2)–(4) as well, then there would be nothing for it but to acknowledge them as persons. That would be simply part and parcel of the "benefit of doubt" aspect of being persons ourselves. But for the present, at any rate, the realization of this prospect seems not merely remote but unrealistic.

Personal Identity

What is it that *individuates* a particular person as such? The self or ego has always been a stumbling block for Western philosophy because of its recalcitrance to finding accommodation within the orthodox framework of substance-ontology. The idea that "the self" is a *thing* (substance), and that whatever occurs in relation to "my mind" and "my thoughts" is accordingly a matter of the activity of a homunculus-like agency of a certain sort (a "mind" substance) is no more than a rather blatant sort of fiction—a somewhat desperate effort to apply the substance-attribute paradigm to a range of phenomena that it just does not fit.

It is, after all, rather repugnant to conceptualize *persons* as *things* (substances)—ourselves above all. Aristotle already bears witness to this difficulty of accommodating within a substance-metaphysic the idea of a self or soul. It is, he tells us, the "substantial form," the *entelechy* of the body. But this stratagem raises more problems than it solves, because the self or soul is so profoundly unlike the other sorts of entelechy examples that Aristotle is able to provide.

People instinctively resist being described in thing-classificatory terms. As Sartre suggests, a wrong-doer may well concede "I did this or that act" but will resist saying "I am a thief," "I am a murderer."[4] Such attributions indicate a fixed nature that we naturally see as repugnant to ourselves. People standardly incline to see themselves and their doings in processual terms as sources of teleological, agency-purposive activities geared to the satisfaction of needs and wants as they appear in the circumstances of the moment. In application to ourselves, at any rate, static thing-classifiers are naturally distasteful.

If one is intent on conceiving of a *person* within the framework of a classical thing-metaphysic, then one is going to be impelled

[4] "Bad Faith," in J. P. Sartre, *Being and Nothingness*, tr. Hazel Barnes (Pocketbook ed., New York, 1966), pp. 107f.

inexorably toward the materialist view that the definitive facet of a person is his or her body and its doings. For of everything that appertains to us, it is clearly one's *body* that is most readily assimilated to the substance paradigm. Think here of David Hume's ventures into self-apprehension:

> From what (experiential) impression could this idea (of *self*) be derived? This question is impossible to answer without a manifest contradiction and absurdity; and yet it is a question which must necessarily be answered, if we would have the idea of self pass for clear and intelligible. . . . For my part, when I enter most intimately into what I call *myself*, I always stumble on some particular perception or other, of heat or cold, light or shade, love or hatred, pain or pleasure. I never can catch *myself* at any time without a perception, and never can observe anything but the perception.[5]

Here Hume is perfectly right. Any such quest for *observational* confrontation with a personal core substance, a self or ego that constitutes the particular person that one is, is destined to end in failure. The only "thing" about ourselves we can get hold of *observationally* is the body and its activities.

However, though we may have difficulties apprehending what we *are*, we have no difficulty experiencing what we *do*. Our bodily and mental activities lie open to experiential apprehension. There is no problem with experiential access to the processes and patterns of process that characterize us personally; our doings and undergoings, either individually or patterned into talents, skills, capabilities, traits, dispositions, habits, inclinations, and tendencies to action and inaction are, after all, what characteristically define the person as the individual he or she is. What makes my experience mine is not some peculiar qualitative character that it exhibits but simply its forming part of the overall ongoing process that defines and constitutes my life. Personal identity is a matter of processual integration.

Once we conceptualize the core "self" of a person as a bundle of actual and potential processes—of action and capacities, tendencies, and dispositions to action (both physical and psychi-

---

[5] *A Treatise of Human Nature*, book 2, part 4, sec. 6, "Of Personal Identity." In the Appendix, Hume further elaborates: "When I turn my reflection on *myself*, I never can perceive this *self* without some one or more perceptions; nor can I ever perceive anything but the perceptions. It is the composition of these, therefore, which forms the SELF."

cal)—then we have a concept of personhood that renders the self or ego experientially accessible, seeing that experiencing itself simply *consists* of such processes. On a process-oriented approach, the self or ego (the constituting core of a person as such, that is, as the particular person he or she is) is simply a megaprocess—a *structured system of processes*. The unity of person is a unity of experience—the coalescence of all of one's diverse microexperiences as parts of one unified macro-process. (It is the same sort of unity of process that links each minute's travel into a single overall journey.) The crux of this approach is the shift in orientation from substance to process—from a unity of hardware, of physical machinery, to a unity of software, of programming or mode of functioning.

Unamuno says that Descartes got it backward, that instead of "cogito, ergo sum res cogitans," one should say, "sum res cogitans, ergo cogito."[6] But this is simply not so. Descartes's reversal of Scholasticism's traditional substantialist perspective is perfectly in order, proceeding from the sound idea that activity comes first ("Im Anfang war die Tat")—that what we do defines what we are. The fundamentality of psychic process for the constitution of a self was put on the agenda of modern philosophy by Descartes.

The salient advantage of this process-geared view of the self as the unfolding of a complex process of "leading a life (of a certain sort)"—with its natural division into a varied manifold subprocesses—is that it does away with the need for a mysterious and experientially inaccessible unifying substantial *object* (on the lines of Kant's "transcendental ego") to constitute a self out of the variety of its experiences. The unity of self comes to be seen as a unity of process—of one large megaprocess that encompasses many smaller ones in its makeup. We arrive at a view of mind that dispenses with the Cartesian homunculus, the "ghost in the machine," and looks to the unity of mind as a unity of functioning—of *operation* rather than *operator*. Such an approach wholly rejects the thing-ontologists' view of a person as an *entity* existing separately from its actions, activities, and experiences. A "self" is viewed not as constituent in terms of a *thing* but as the product of a process-engendered identity.

[6] *Del sentimiento trágico*, p. 52.

On this basis, the Humean complaint that one experiences feeling this and doing that, but never experiences oneself is much like the complaint of the person who says, "I see him picking up that brick, and mixing that batch of mortar, and troweling that brick into place, but I never see him building a wall." Even as "building the wall" just exactly is the complex process that is *composed* of those various activities of putting on now this brick, now that one, so—from the process point of view—one's self just is the complex process *composed* of those various physical and psychic experiences and actions in their systemic interrelationship. A person is as a person does. What individuates us as persons, then, is something processual—namely, *the way or manner* in which we carry on those salient processes (intelligence, rational agency, self-assertion, and social reciprocity) that constitute the defining core of personhood.

The Obligations of Personhood

The characteristic thing about a person is being an intelligent free agent endowed with self-understanding and self-esteem. It is people's potential for rational agency that makes them people as such. But why should we humans strive to realize this potential? Why should we comport ourselves as rational agents who align and coordinate their beliefs, actions, and evaluations under the guidance of reason?

The answer is straightforward. We ought to comport ourselves rationally because rationality is an essential part of our self-definition as persons. Rationality thus represents a crucial aspect of our deepest self-interest—our being able to maintain a proper sense of legitimacy and self-worth by being able to see ourselves as the sorts of creatures we claim to be.

It is through this fundamental *ontological* imperative that mere counsels of reason are transmuted into commands—commands issued by one side of our nature (the rational) to ourselves at large. We have to do here with an injunction issued by the authoritative part of ourselves to the whole. Our claim to be rational free agents of itself establishes our position in the world's scheme of things, with the result that rationality becomes a matter of duty for us, of ontological obligation.

Francis Hutcheson saw morality as a matter of so acting that we can reflectively approve of our own character—of so acting that one need make no excuses for oneself toward oneself.[7] But in much the same way, the fundamental ontological impetus to self-development is a matter of acting in the light of what sort of person one ought to be—of so comporting oneself that one can unhesitantly approve of oneself as being that which one has, through one's own actions, made of oneself. No one is closer to us than our own self (*egomet mihi sum proximus*), and being on good terms with ourselves is perhaps the most fundamental and basic real and true interest that we have. The ontological imperative toward self-realization—and the rational and moral imperatives it carries in its wake—are simply part and parcel of this fundamental impetus and commandment. Our deepest nature calls on us to be on good terms with ourselves and thus, in turn, requires due heed of our rationality. What is at stake is our very identity as beings of the sort we do and should see ourselves as being.

The crux of the imperative to personhood is thus the fundamental duty to make good use of the opportunities that come our way to realize ourselves as fully as possible—the fundamental duty of self-realization. Insofar as one "owes" it to anyone at all, one owes this duty to oneself and to "the world at large" or, at any rate, to the community of rational agents within it. The duty at issue is a duty at once to oneself and to the general scheme of things that brought one forth to develop one's highest potential as the kind of creature one is—or deems to be. It roots in the imperatives: "Realize your highest potential as the sort of being you are!" and "Develop as best you can your own possibilities for the best." This fundamental ontological duty of self-realization appertains to any rational agent whatsoever. Any agent as such stands committed to enhance and realize its own best potentialities, such self-realization being the point of confluence where self-interest and obligation flow together.

To be sure, rational agency is not programmed into us like an animal's instinct. We are free creatures. And as such we do well to walk in the paths of reason not because considerations of necessity dictate that we must, but because considerations of desir-

[7] *A System of Moral Philosophy* (Glasgow, 1775).

ability indicate that this affords the greatest real advantage for us as the sort of creatures we are.

The ontological aspect is crucial here. If personhood were *merely* and *only* a matter of (true) prudence and self-interest (however much it is our *real* interests that are at stake), then its worth would be less than it is. We do—and must—value our personhood, not just because it helps to feather our nest, but because we see it as a crucial component of our very nature as the sort of beings we are—or, better, take ourselves to be. The crux of our mandatory commitment to personhood lies in the region where axiology and ontology meet—in the value that it has for us as the salient feature that determines our place in the world's scheme of things.

Good Advice

ADVICE is one of the most common commodities in the modern world. Like the very air we breathe, it surrounds us on every side. Advice comes to us invited or uninvited—from our friends and relations, from teachers and professional counselors of every description, from politicians and public figures, from the media, from publications of all sorts, and on and on.

But despite the vast quantities of advice given, little attention has been paid to the underlying issue of what the giving of advice is all about. The theoretical aspects of advice are seldom examined: the conception of advice is not something that has particularly engaged the attention of theorists. The terms at issue (advice, counsel, recommendation, and their foreign language equivalents, *consilium, monitum, conseil, Ratschlag,* etc.) do not even figure in philosophical dictionaries. The practice of advice-giving may be common, but the study of the practice is certainly not so. The present discussion offers a very small contribution to filling this very large gap.

Some Distinctions

To begin with, it is important to distinguish between advice or counsel on the one hand and commands or orders on the other. In the *Summa Theologica,* Thomas Aquinas sensibly observed that "a commitment implies obligation, whereas a counsel is left to the option of the one to whom it is given."[1] A command is imperative and definitely binding—its instructions are framed in the imperatival language of "you must." A counsel, by contrast, is advisory and offers a recommendation governed by the formula, "you are well advised to do it"—its instructions are framed in the recommendatory language of "you should."

To be sure, both commands and counsels involve an element of direction. But commands simply demand ("you must"), while advice has to convince ("you should"). The imperatival impetus of a command lies in the *power* of the commanding authority, while the imperatival impetus of advice roots in a *rational principle*. In ignoring or going against valid orders, one creates problems for someone else's agenda—generally someone in a position to make one regret that one has done so. But in ignoring or going against good advice, one undermines an agenda that is, or should be, one's own. Orders can be given in ways that are otherwise reasonless, simply to manifest the commander's authority and power. But sound advice must always be something one can back with reasons—and indeed reasons that (insofar as sound) pivot on the interests of the recipient. Because of this persuasive dimension, it is a salient and definitive feature of genuinely *good* advice that it must always hinge on the best interests of the advisee who is its recipient.

Advice can differ in *scope*, and it is useful to distinguish between special-purpose advice and general-purpose advice. Special-purpose advice is directed at particular groups of people—to the lovelorn, or homeowners, or princes. General-purpose advice, by contrast, is addressed to everyone at large; its audience is universal. Aspiring pianists are well advised to practice their instruments daily, but we all are well advised to take proper care of our health or to develop some of our talents and skills.

Advice can be hypothetical or categorical. Hypothetical advice is geared to one's particular idiosyncratic aims—one's own characteristic goals and purposes. IF you want to be an engineer, THEN you should study calculus, and IF you want to be a good actor, THEN you should watch able performers closely to learn from them. By contrast, categorical advice is unconditional:

[1] Aquinas, Q14, a. 1.

"Avoid acting so as to defeat your own purposes" or "Never offend people needlessly." Such advice is appropriate irrespective of one's particular needs—or, if you prefer—is geared to ends that all of us *ought* to have, irrespective of what our particular wants or desires actually happen to be. The issue of the merits or demerits of merely special-purpose or hypothetical advice is a matter of means-ends rationality. It hinges on the strictly factual issue of the efficacy of the proposed means to the designated ends. The issue of the quality of universally categorical advice is something very different, however. It is a matter of the rationality of ends—of the intrinsic value and inherent merit of the positivities at issue.

There are three major modes of advice, prudential, beneficial, and moral. Their character is as follows:

1. *Prudential*: advice geared to what somebody wants, that is, to satisfying the person's particular (contingent) wishes and desires;

2. *Beneficial*: advice geared to what is good for someone, that is, to what is in the person's "real" and "true" self-interest, to satisfying *genuine* needs and *appropriate* wants (irrespective of what the person's actual wishes and desires may happen to be);

3. *Moral*: advice geared to what one *ought* to do (morally), to what is the right thing to do.

With prudence, *desire* is the key: the pivot is the purely factual matter of a person's wants and wishes. The crux of beneficial advice is the normative issue of what a person *ought* to want because of its being really and truly to his or her benefit. And moral advice turns not on what people can do to serve their own best interests, but on what they ought to do to protect and respect the interests of others. (It is clear on this basis that the three regions will overlap in various ways.)

Prudential and beneficial advice are both self-regarding; moral advice, by contrast, is fundamentally other-regarding. Beneficial and moral advice are geared not to the particular *ends or purposes* that a person contingently happens to have; they are normative in being geared to the *values* that any (rational and reasonable) person *ought* to have, given the nature of his or her best interests.

It is important in this context to avoid confusing self-regard with selfishness. For being *selfish*, in standard usage, is a matter of doing what advantages you specifically *at the expense of others*. In this regard, Ayn Rand's influential advocacy of "the virtue of selfishness" is badly flawed in its acknowledged reluctance to distinguish between outright *selfishness* and mere *prudence*, the sensible concern for one's best interests.[2] (Concern for the welfare of one's children, for example, is self-interested, but there is nothing selfish about it.) In *expounding* her doctrine that selfishness is a virtue, Rand gives it shock value by speaking of *selfishness*, but in *defending* it she sensibly pivots the matter on a prudent and proper concern for one's own genuine best interests.

The Quality of Advice

Advice is always teleological—aimed at the realization of an end of some sort—although these ends can be thematically varied (wants, interests, obligations). The appropriate appraisal categories for assessing the merit of advice are not *true* and *false* (as with beliefs or statements) or *right* and *wrong* (as with actions or evaluations), but *good* and *bad*. Good advice leads effectively toward the realization of appropriate goals; bad advice is unproductive in this regard. Advice operates in the region of means to ends. And the quality of those ends is something that is crucial to the goodness of advice.

It emerges in this light that advice qualifies as being good if following it will lead (or is comparatively likely to lead) its recipient to the thematically appropriate result, that is,

in the case of *prudential* advice, to what one wants;
in the case of *beneficial* advice, to what is good for one's best interest; and
in the case of *moral* advice, to what duly protects the best interests of others.

What distinguishes good advice is thus its manifest efficiency and effectiveness in realizing the particular thematic value at issue (prudence, benefit, morality). Being well intentioned is emphatically *not* sufficient to render advice good.

[2] See Ayn Rand, *The Virtue of Selfishness: A New Concept of Egoism* (New York, 1964).

The principled nature of good advice sets it apart in nature from recommendations that look good because of sheer luck. "Beware the ides of March," the old crone called to Julius Caesar, and no doubt as his funeral procession passed by a few days later, she muttered "I told you so." But it would not be appropriate to say that she gave him good advice. Advice that, with the wisdom of hindsight, we wish we had followed does not thereby automatically qualify as good advice. Grounds and reasons figure pivotally in assessing the merit of advice.

This also explains why there is something impersonal and general about good advice. Rationality is the key here: to act rationally is to do what *anybody* is well advised to do *in the particular circumstances*. Whatever considerations render it rational for someone to do some particular thing will ipso facto render it rational for anyone else who is "in his shoes."

Unfortunately, the worst judge of good advice is often its addressee. For, unlike any detached bystander, the recipient of advice frequently cannot properly assess it at the time, in the heat of battle, so to speak. The quality of advice is something that all too frequently becomes apparent to the recipient only in distant retrospect, with a newfound detachment and the wisdom of hindsight.

It is thus by no means the case that those who receive good advice generally welcome it. In the case of beneficial and moral advice, this is all too evident. But it holds for prudential advice as well. We want something very much over the long run. But the good advice to forgo more immediate and pressing lesser desiderata for the sake of achieving that end may be far from pleasing. Often the giver of good advice is no more welcome than the bearer of bad tidings, as those dealing with family members who are on a diet soon come to realize.

This question of what we would do if we were "in someone else's shoes" of course raises the issue of just what are we to take along when we step into those shoes? If we take *nothing* of our own along, then we are bound to see the issue exactly as that recipient does—there is no other possibility. If we take *everything* along, then of course the recipient simply vanishes from the scene—his idiosyncratic wants and needs count for nothing. What we have to do to proceed realistically is to assess what it would be appropriate to do in conditions "sufficient like" his, specifically what it would be intelligent to do in the light of his situation and *of his* information. It is *not* a matter of changing the rules of the game on our subject, but one of assessing how well he plays the game by *his* rules—the rules he follows, or rather that he ought to be following, given his valid needs and real interests. For example, only the agent himself can tell *exactly* how he wants to apportion resources, concern, and attention between the immediate present, the near future, and the distant future—though general principles may set limits. (The person who discounts one of these timespans almost completely is not being sensible.) What we take along, then, when we put ourselves into another's shoes is not our *values*, but our native intelligence and our "common sense"—our ability to think and to judge as sensible people. However, the various substantive commitments on matters of fact and of value are things that we must in large measure take over from the agent at issue.

Responsibility always lies with the person who *accepts* advice. The recipient can never deflect recrimination by saying, "but I only did what X advised." Clearly, one does not automatically act wisely in following a putative expert's advice unless due care has been exercised to ascertain that the adviser is indeed knowledgeable about the matter at issue. The decision to seek, accept, and implement advice is such that a recipient always bears responsibility. And this basic ground rule means that in offering *advice*—rather, say, than commands—the advice-giver acknowledges the autonomy of the recipient.

As indicated above, something inherently universal always lies at the basis of good advice. The advice that helps you to be a good doctor or lawyer is object-specific. But the ultimate principle at issue is: "Find a way of earning your livelihood that enables you to develop your talents, to derive pleasure for your endeavors, and to contribute usefully to the work of your society." And this is something universal. Sound specific-purpose advice must always ultimately root in sound general-purpose advice.

Accordingly, the *principles* on which good advice proceeds are universal. You may, in your particular circumstance, be well advised to ask your friend Robert for a loan. This matter of concrete procedure is something that is geared to your particular situation. But at the level of fundamentals, *anybody* is well advised to try to obtain by honest means the funds required to meet a pressing need. Good advice must always instantiate some principles of universal applicability, since all people share those *fundamental* interests in which our differential interests take root.

The fact that good advice must always be grounded in underlying principles of potentially general application means that good advice is something that is *objective*. There is no advising people about purely subjective matters—no one can advise you about what flavors of ice cream you like. But other people certainly can advise you about objective matters—about what is good for you to eat, for example, or about what foods a person of your physiological makeup is apt to find tasty. This is precisely why decision-makers have a staff of "advisers," and why the principle "two heads are better than one" is sensible. Advice is a multilateral affair—the verb "to counsel" stands correlative with the noun "a council," that is, a group of wise heads that is in the business of providing good advice.

The Literature of Advice: Prudential

The published literature of advice in its various forms deserves closer notice. A visit to any good bookstore suffices to indicate that the literature of *prudential* advice is endlessly variegated. There are cookbooks, books of etiquette, and "how-to" books of all sorts affording guidance in everything from building furniture to writing love letters. The numerous treatises on princeship before and after Machiavelli are a classical example of this category. A more contemporary example is the profusion of diet books instructing people how to eat for slimmer appearance or greater longevity. Such books lavish advice for the realization of particular contingent objectives that are widely current in our society.

A classic in the field of prudential advice is Dale Carnegie's *How to Win Friends and Influence People,* an all-time international best-seller whose sales continue going strong over fifty years after its initial publication. Lacing its commonsense advice with informative anecdotes and the obiter dicta of well-known achievers, the whole book exemplifies its own paramount advice to see things from the other person's point of view. What the reader doubtless wants to hear is that by following a handful of relatively painless and plausible rules, he or she too can succeed in interpersonal relations. And this is exactly what the author provides—to the satisfaction of his audience and the profit of his publishers.

Of course, most people want not only friends and influence but also money. And here too the how-to literature does not let them down. The all-time success story in this field is Napoleon Hill's deservedly celebrated book *Think and Grow Rich*. Hill's analysis of what is needed for achieving wealth—or indeed one's paramount desire in general—is not only sensible but realistic in its recognition of the difficulties to be surmounted and its stress on the substantial personal price one must pay in surmounting them.

As one browses in bookshops one is led to recognize the literature of prudential advice for what it is: an enormous, and, unsurprisingly, an enormously profitable industry.

The Literature of Advice: Beneficial

Prudential advice presupposes a given fixed aim, a predesignated desire (getting rich, governing successfully). Beneficial advice, by contrast, does not take its advisees' wants and desires as fixed givens. Rather, it has a more elevated, "consciousness-raising" objective—to awaken in the advisees a more sophisticated and developed sense of what's worth wanting—of what it would be good for them to bother about.

What is at issue here need not, however, be anything as lofty as cultural edification. Even guide books and travel books afford an example. In pointing out what is *worth* seeing, what any "sensible" person would be foolish to miss, they do not gear themselves blindly to our prevailing desires but manifest a concern for what is for our good.

A more characteristic example is afforded by the large and ever-growing literature on planning for what are euphemistically called "the golden years"—the period of life after seventy that all of us eventually reach barring the intervention of uncooperative Fate. We all know the sorts of recommendations that are made—keep up friendships, get new experiences through travel, cultivate interests, develop hobbies, and the like. Such suggestions reflect the ample experience of our predecessors in dealing with an issue that every human confronts with advancing years. In this regard the issue reflects the inherent universality of beneficial advice.

The definitive thing about beneficial advice is that it is not restrained to seeing a person's established wants (desires, wishes) as the sole—let alone paramount—reason for action. Its concern is for the *appropriate* ends that a sensible agent *ought* to have given the nature of his or her best interests. The crux is not what one *does* want but what one *would want if*—if one were really sensible, if "one's head were screwed on right."

The Literature of Advice: Moral

Last but not least, let us consider the literature of *moral* advice. Its cardinal aim, as Aristotle already maintained,[3] is to guide us in becoming good people. Since this is something that is in everyone's real or true best interests, moral advice can in fact be regarded as a (particularly important) sector or department of beneficial advice, and the moralists of ancient Greece were generally inclined to see it in this light.

At first thought, it may appear strange that the literature of explicit moral advice is so small. There is, of course, a very substantial philosophical literature on the various second-order issues—on the *nature* of morality (what makes actions moral?) and on the *rationale* of morality (why be moral?). But there is surprisingly little if anything in the way of moral handbooks or guidebooks—philosophical or otherwise—on the first-order issue of just what it is that one ought morally speaking to do.

Of course, every society has its lore and literature of admonitory anecdotes and stories to convey object lessons of moral behavior (think of Aesop's fables or of George Washington and the cherry tree). But no one bothers to compile theses that explicitly formulate the general principles on which moral advice is based. ("One should not hurt people's feelings needlessly.") There is a ramified literature of how-to books on matters of etiquette (think of Emily Post or Amy Vanderbilt). But their counterparts by way of moral guidebooks are notable for their absence. There is no comparable how-to literature to codify the ground-level prin-

---

[3] *Nicomachean Ethics*, II, 2.

ciples of moral comportment. The reason for this phenomenon is not far to seek. Moral advice requires literary disguise. It is acceptable if formulated in fables or parables, in stories or proverbs. But if openly paraded in the form of explicit theses and principles, it seems incredibly boring and banal. The ground-level precepts of moral advice are too trite for explicit codification—they are things we learn, if ever, at our mother's knee. Explicit moral advice is simply too basic for adults: even if the book existed, few would feel comfortable enough about acquiring it to confront a sales clerk or a check-out librarian.

Moral advice is thus particularly unwelcome to its recipients, and is a paradigm instance of something that it is more blessed to give than to receive. Exactly because morality is something that everyone is generally presumed to have learned in childhood, it seems an insult to one's intelligence to be given moral lessons in later life.

The Pursuit of Happiness

Is the happiness of the recipient and his near and dear the basis of all good advice? Various theorists tell us that the "pursuit of happiness" constitutes the be-all and end-all of human existence. But this surely distorts the actual solution. Sensible parents invariably want their children to be happy, of course, but also—among other things—morally *good* and *productive* in contributing to the world's stock of human achievements. One would not want one's children—and one should not want one-self—to be happy at the price of moral depravity or personal sloth. ("Better Socrates dissatisfied than a pig satisfied," John Stuart Mill quite rightly said.) A truly *satisfying* life—a life whose bearer is entitled to rational satisfaction with what has been done and achieved—is not one that is predicated on happiness alone. Other salient factors—virtue, productiveness, etc.—must enter in.

There are, or certainly should be, important goals beyond personal happiness, goals whose attainment, or even pursuit, makes for a fuller and a better person. Examples of such goals include gaining the respect of one's associates and the love of some among them; pride of achievement in some area of activity, vocational or avocational; appreciation of the accomplishments of the race in art and science; and the enjoyment of hobbies or sports. These goals all revolve about the theme of self-development and fulfillment, a capitalizing on the opportunities for the realization of a person's potential for appreciating and contributing to the instructive impetus of the human spirit. The achievement of such goals lays the basis for a legitimate view of oneself as a unit of worth: a *person* in the fullest sense. And a significant and general lack in these regards is indicative, not necessarily of any diminution of "happiness," but of an impoverishment of spirit. In consequence, people as individuals have (i.e., can, should, and—in general—do have) a wide spectrum of "transcendent" *goals* that lie above and beyond the sphere of their own happiness. For individuals (and also societies), these "transcendent" goals count: they have a validity, legitimacy, and importance all their own.

Since the heyday of utilitarianism in the first part of the nineteenth century, the thesis that the maximization of personal happiness—along with its composite cousin, the general welfare—is the ultimate pivot of social philosophy has gained widespread currency, even to the point of attaining the status of dogma. To adopt this view, however, is to overlook something very basic: the inherent incompleteness of happiness in relation to valid human goals at large. For beyond the hedonic sector of human happiness, there is also, and most significantly, the whole artistic sector of man's higher goals and aspirations. No matter how we shape in its details our overarching vision of the good life for man, happiness will play only a partial and subsidiary role, because a person (or a society) can be happy, healthy, prosperous, and the like, and yet lack all those resources of personality, intellect, and character that, like the cultivation of the mind and the fostering of human congeniality, can make life rich, full, and meaningful. The range of legitimate human values transcends that of happiness alone.

Toward people or nations that have—even to abundance—the constituents of happiness, we may feel envy, but our *admiration* and *respect* could never be won on this ground alone. An entire dimension of legitimate human desiderata lies beyond welfare, indeed even beyond the realm of happiness as such. For there are many things that give people (or, nations) *satisfaction*—perfectly legitimate satisfaction—without rendering them any *happier*. The reader of biographies cannot but become convinced that there are full and satisfying lives—eminently worth-while lives—that are not particularly happy, but shot through with the "quiet desperation" that Thoreau perhaps mistakenly imputes to most of us. And contrariwise, there are happy lives that are deplorable and may well be deemed so (quite rightly) by the people who "enjoy" them. The important point is not to dwell on these lugubrious facets of the human situation, but to stress one relatively simple and straightforward point: that any adequate vision of "the good life" for people—and for socie-ties—must reckon with areas of human achievement wholly outside the domain of "happiness." The central concept of this excellence-oriented, "transcendent" domain is *quality*, particu-larly in the realization of human potentialities for the realization of value. Excellence, dignity, and the sense of worth are the leading themes throughout. Neither for individual nor for so-cieties is "the pursuit of happiness" the sole and legitimate guide to action; its dictates must be counterbalanced by recog-nizing the importance of doing those things that we can look back on, in after years, with justifiable pride.

Right-minded individuals are concerned not only with hap-piness but also with *self-realization*, with "what they make of themselves" and "what sort of life they lead," acknowledging an inalienable obligation to foster the *quality* of their lives. One can realize one's highest potential only by setting one's sights on goals that go far beyond issues of personal happiness. Sensible people see this as a matter of self-image, self-realization, self-identity, and just plain pride. What is at issue here is not a *utili-tarian* defense in terms of happiness alone, but an *"idealistic"* de-fense in terms of the realization of human values and ideals—an appreciation that happiness without ideals and values can prove to be corruptive and debilitating.

Such deliberations serve to indicate that it is emphatically wrong to maintain that promoting happiness is the sole and soli-tary function for good advice. These "transcendent" goals also deserve their due place in the realm of evaluative considerations.

The Problem of Interaction

Advice, as we have seen, is always offered from a particular thematic point of view—be it prudential or beneficial or moral. But what of the interrelationship of these categories of advice?

Are they ultimately distinct and co-equal domains, or is one of them somehow paramount and predominant over the rest?

This is a question that can only be answered on the basis of a comprehensive view of the nature of man. For to resolve this issue of thematic priority we have first to ask ourselves some rather fundamental questions regarding the values at issue with human existence. We have to attempt a visualization of what people can and should be. All this is a tall order. For the present, we shall be pretty dogmatic about it, nailing our flag to the position favored by the moral theorists of Greek antiquity, who held that what is primary and predominant is the beneficial standpoint—what is good for a person in terms of his own overall best interests.

The line of thought to which the Greek moralists inclined ran roughly as follows. The beneficial predominates over the prudential because what a person *wants* will only be proper and appropriate—is only something that ultimately he *ought* to have—if the objective in question is something that is actually good for him. And the beneficial standpoint "predominates" over the moral because it in fact *encompasses* it. A person who fails to be moral thereby damages his own best interests because he thereby manages to injure himself in undermining the self-respect that is a free rational agent's due. On this perspective, then, the beneficial point of view—oriented at a person's own true or best or real interests—emerges as the ultimate basis for any and all good advice.

Self-Optimization as Paramount

What should be said of someone who seeks advice, receives good advice that he himself acknowledges as such, and then does not follow it? Given that a defect of intellect is not at issue (since, by hypothesis, the person understands the advice and acknowledges its merit), the fault at issue is clearly a deficiency of will of some sort, be it through weakness or perversity. Clearly, then, such a person lays himself open to reproach and recrimination.

We humans can, do, and should see ourselves as members of the special category of *persons*—of free rational agents, a group that may, conceivably, extend beyond the population of this planet. And as beings of this sort, we are in substantial measure self-made: we are the sort of creatures we are in virtue of the sorts of aspirations we have, the kind of creatures we see ourselves as actually or potentially being. *Homo sapiens* is capable of at least partial self-construction—able to make himself into the sort of being he ought (ontologically considered) to be, given the opportunities afforded him through this world's arrangements.

The ignoring of good advice thus automatically carries a natural sanction in its wake—the onus of irrationality. The eminently appropriate injunction, "Be an authentic human being!," comes down to this: do the utmost to become the sort of rational and responsible creature that a human person, at best or most, is capable of being. "Be the best you can be—become what you ought!" So runs a basic rational imperative to self-optimization that impels an intelligent agent to make effective use of its opportunities to cultivate its potential for the good. And in this regard, wastefulness is wicked. For an intelligent agent to stunt its potential through its own deliberate action or inaction is both profoundly irrational and fundamentally *wrong*. We have only one chance at life, and letting its opportunities for the good slip by is a shameful loss—regrettable alike from the standpoint of the world's interests and our own.

This existential obligation—predicated on our being committed to certain goods and goals simply in virtue of our being the sort of creature that we actually or potentially are—is the ultimate basis of all sound beneficial advice. Self-optimization—the realization of one's highest and best potential—is the paramount benefit for any rational creature. For in ignoring its call we effectively deprive ourselves of a paramount good through our own deliberate action. And to do this is something profoundly irrational precisely because reason enjoins us to the intelligent cultivation of our own best or real interests. The definitive character of good advice is that it guides us toward being what we can and should ideally be—individuals who realize as fully as possible their human potential for being rational agents.

FOUR

Proverbial Wisdom

PHILOSOPHERS generally draw on the texts of other philosophers as a source of material for their contemplation of human affairs, reacting to views about life and the world that are found in the deliberations of their learned congeners. And this is understandable enough. After all, people in general almost never trouble to formulate and defend their views of life on paper, setting them out in a form available to others for examination and critical appraisal. Still, the matter does not rest altogether on this footing. True enough, ordinary people do not produce bodies of written reflection expounding their views of life. But other roads lead into their avenues of thought. In particular, a communal group's proverbial dicta provide us with a window into life as seen by ordinary people—an insight into the philosophical outlook of a silent majority that would otherwise remain mute because philosophy, literature, scholarship, and other modes of written expression remain outside its range.[1]

By common dictionary definition, a proverb is a popular maxim that pithily conveys a useful lesson or instruction. The three salient factors of a proverb are thus instructiveness, brevity, and

[1] Collections of proverbs have always been popular. In the 15th century, Polydore Vergil brought out in Paris a collection of Greek and Roman proverbs, and by the time Erasmus completed his *Adagia* in the 1530's, he had more than 4,000 entries. See N. Z. Davis, "Proverbial Wisdom and Popular Errors," in *Society and Culture in Early Modern France* (Stanford, Calif., 1975), pp. 233–34.

popularity.[2] And its reason for being is to provide useful guidance in the conduct of life. Perhaps we can learn but little from this source of "popular philosophy," but that little is neither uninstructive nor uninteresting. For the proverbs of a people show us how they really think about things.

Proverbs

Proverbs are generally anonymous, passed down from time immemorial. Sometimes, however, the dictum of an identifiable individual becomes proverbial—as, for example, Sir Robert Walpole's cynical remark now familiarly rendered as "Every man has his price."

Proverbial wisdom is overwhelmingly concerned with the conduct of life, formulating the "commonsense" lessons that put at the disposal of everyone the hard-won wisdom of the sagacious. (After all, "Lo que hace el loco a la postre, hace el sabio al principio.") Hence the bulk of it is devoted to rules and instructions ("When in Rome, do as the Romans do"). To be sure, proverbs are sometimes framed in the form of questions. But then questions are rhetorical and do duty for an injunction. ("Quis custodiet ipsos custodes?": one has to trust *somebody*. "But who is to bell the cat?": be practical about your proposals and ensure their implementability.) Here, as elsewhere, the exception tests (not *proves*, save in an antiquated sense of the term) the rule: Exceptio probat regulam.

Proverbial wisdom's messages are generally universal. In overwhelming measure, proverbs reflect constancies of the human condition and not cultural peculiarities of particular groups or eras: Plus ça change, plus c'est la même chose. Virtually every proverb has equivalents in other languages: Let's cross that bridge when we get to it / Kommt Zeit, kommt Rat; Mutter treu wird taeglich neu / Tendresse maternelle se toujours renouvelle; The devil too may quote scripture / Con l'evangelo se diverta eretico; Don't look a gift horse in the mouth / Si quis dat mannus, ne quaere in dentibus annos; A bird in hand is worth more

---

[2] In principle, the populace at issue in "popularity" might merely be a particular group (as for example *Traduttori, traditori* is addressed to scholars). But the present discussion will focus on what is popular in the wider sense.

than two in the bush / Una avis in dextra, melior quam quattuor extra. The basic message is generally universal, although the particular mode of expression may be culturally shaped in ways that call for backward information about prevailing conditions: the English ridicule taking coal to Newcastle, the Greeks taking owls to Athens, the Indians taking pepper to Hindustan. Sometimes, however, closely kindred proverbs move off in somewhat different directions. "When it rains, it pours" means once troubles begin for someone, he or she has lots of them. But "Cuando llueve, todos se mojan" means once troubles begin for someone, many people are affected.

The Structure of Proverbial Wisdom

Proverbial wisdom for the most part falls into a mere handful of thematic categories:

1. Injunctions to prudence and caution in human interactions: Caveat emptor; Better safe than sorry.

2. Injunctions to avoid vice and cultivate virtue and probity: Pride goeth before a fall; Honesty is the best policy; Let your word be your bond.

3. Injunctions to sagacious self-interest: Carpe diem; You can't take it with you; Quien a dos señores ha de servir, al uno ha de mentir.

4. Encouragements to action or effort: A rolling stone gathers no moss; Nothing ventured, nothing gained; Ce n'est que le premier pas qui coute; Delay is the road to never.

5. Advice for maintaining health and well-being: Im Becher ersaufen mehr als im Meere; Mas mató la cena que sanó Avicena.

6. Maxims on managing family interactions and affairs: Honor thy father and thy mother; Blood is thicker than water.

7. Advice on managing dealings with people: In vino veritas; Never trust a man who can't look you straight in the eye; Verbum sat sapienti est.

8. Sayings about keeping expectations within "realistic" bounds: A cat has nine lives (but you don't); Non omnia possumus omnes; You can't squeeze blood from a turnip.

9. Reminders of human shortcomings: A tout heure, femme

pleure; El rio pasado, el santo olivadado; Where the carcass is, there will the vultures be gathered together (Matt. 24:28).

10. Adages providing excuses—for the success of others, for example: Among the blind, the one-eyed is king; having "the luck of the Irish."

This list of basic thematic categories can be lengthened—but not very far.

A Lesson

Proverbs are intended to provide us with guidance for life. But life is complex. No simple rules are satisfactory; an approach or procedure that works in some cases will fail miserably in others. So proverbial wisdom has to be attuned to move in either direction in line with the almost infinitely complex and ramified character of different circumstances and situations. If there is to be any body of simple rules at all, it must, if adequate, be prepared to move in opposite directions subject to the indications of diversified circumstances.

The most striking and significant feature of proverbial wisdom is its inconsistency. It is Janus-faced in its tendency to look in opposite directions at once, reminiscent of Newton's first law, in that for every proverb of one tendency there is another with equal force of the opposite tendency, as attested by the following pairs: A stitch in time saves nine / Look before you leap; Beware of Greeks bearing gifts / Don't look a gift horse in the mouth; Look after the pennies and the pounds will look after themselves / You can't take it with you; Plus ça change, plus c'est la même chose / Tempora mutantar, nos et mutatur in illis.

This inconsistency among opposed proverbs is not simply a matter of the superficial inconsistency of conventional expressions. If Tom "died a thousand deaths" when Jane appeared at his party, obviously he did not die at all. Again, when a young couple is said to be "married without benefit of clergy," it is clear that they live together without being married. But proverbial inconsistency is something deeper than rhetorical paradox. Proverbs that point in opposite directions mark the complexity of human life: that there is a time to hurry ("A stitch in time saves nine") and a time for being slow ("Haste makes waste"); that "depending on conditions," both ways of proceeding are proper and well advised.

This inconsistency explains why in the end proverbial wisdom is unsatisfying as a basis for philosophy. Philosophers see rational coherence as a prime desideratum. They are engaged in a constant struggle for coherence that forces one to abandon a part of what one wants in the interests of overall consistency. The inconsistency of proverbial wisdom is a luxury that philosophy cannot afford.

The Illuminating Nature of Proverbs

Proverbial wisdom almost invariably deals with the invariant universals of human life, addressing the shared needs and desires of people always and everywhere. Its characteristic themes— virtue and sin, prudence and folly, family, social interaction, and the rest—represent constants of the human condition that affect us all, always and everywhere. But though invariant, those universals are still subject to variable emphases. Changing context and circumstances make for changing priorities. With varying conditions there is a wider scope and greater need for one or another of such opposed factors as caution/daring; thrift/ liberality; deliberation/action; and conformity/going one's own way. And with variation in these factors comes a variability in the appropriateness of proverbs.

Accordingly, an analysis of the thematic tendency of current appeals to proverbial wisdom can be an illuminating exercise, reflecting the priorities and values of a particular society in its time and place. The prominence of proverbs of a particular orientation is an important index to the prevailing "climate of thought," for as Francis Bacon rightly observed, "The genius, wit, and spirit of a nation are discovered in its proverbs." It is certainly suggestive that in contemporary America the use of proverbs of a relativistic tendency is particularly prominent ("Live and let live," "To each his own"), whereas in the day of the founding fathers, the Protestant Ethic reflected in the homely sayings of Benjamin Franklin's *Poor Richard's Almanac* were in great fashion ("The rolling stone gathers no moss," "Early to bed and early to rise . . ."). The proverbs that are popular at a particular juncture provide suggestive information about a society's circumstances. A period ruled by "birds of a feather flock together" can hardly be as appealing as one where "no mind is so empty but that one can take something from it" is prominent. In its revelations about the "popular philosophy" of an era, the register of a society's popular proverbs also tells us a good deal about the quality of its life.

Proverbial wisdom is the plain man's surrogate for philosophy. Its ubiquity says something about the inescapability of philosophy—its ability to penetrate even where *theorists* cannot gain entry. And its inherent inconsistency shows that here too, at the pre- or subtheoretical level, philosophy is also beset by that internal dissonance and conflict that is so striking a feature of the discussions of the learned. Omar Khayyám cuttingly reproves the quarrelsomeness of the learned:

> Myself when young did eagerly frequent
> Doctor and Saint, and heard great Argument
>   About it and about: but evermore
> Came out by the same Door as in I went.[3]

Proverbial wisdom shows that the situation of the plain man is in this regard no different from that of the learned. The vexatious and oft-lamented diversity of opinions that surrounds us on all sides—in philosophy and in everyday life alike—is simply part and parcel of the human condition.

[3] *Rubáiyát of Omar Khayyám*, tr. Edward Fitzgerald (London, 1859), poem XXVII.

FIVE

Age and the Stages of Life

AN EIGHT-YEAR-OLD girl does not normally and naturally say to herself: "I am just a child." And a man of advanced years is not inclined to say of himself: "I am an old man."[1] We do not ordinarily tend to think of ourselves or of those particularly near and dear to us in such age-classificatory terms. Rather, we ordinarily think of people close to us as *individuals* playing certain age-unaffected functional roles ("my mother," "my uncle," "my child") and possessed of certain perduring characteristics, abilities, and dispositions. At family reunions, we sort ourselves into functionally generational strata ("the grandparents," "the cousins"), which often combine people across a considerable span of years. We deem ourselves and those near to us too special to stand in need of classification in the domain of age or social class or intelligence or personality type.

Years as such are not all that important for us—what matters primarily is how they relate us to others. Generally, we incline to look on ourselves as a very special case indeed—as defining the reference point around which other cases are positioned. One of the most basic questions we humans ask in our encounters with other people is, "Is he or she older or younger than I am?" We tend to see the crucial issue in terms of people's relationship to

[1] In fact, only about 10 percent of white Americans aged 65 consider themselves old, and the figure is still a low 30 percent among 70-year-olds. James E. Birren and K. Warner Schaie, eds., *Handbook of the Psychology of Aging*, 2d ed. (New York, 1985), p. 62.

ourselves: an "old" person is not someone who has attained a certain age, but someone who is, say, fifteen years older than we are. (An ever-receding horizon seems to separate us from old age: to the young child, someone in his twenties is old; to the 60-year-old, it is someone above 75.)

But self-referential description has its limits—especially in circumstances where the self keeps changing. For communicative purposes we cannot let the matter rest there. Accordingly, no language lacks the age-classifying terminology of young and old, child and adult. Markedly distinct stages are at issue, and changing planning horizons come into play. Children "have their whole lives before them" and tend to think that they will go on forever. The young live in a thought-world of unimpeded possibilities—as exemplified in teen-age "daydreaming." The middle-aged inhabit a world of action and activity (of "making their way in the world") and are attracted to the carpe diem outlook characteristic of midlife crises. For the elderly approaching the end of their potential, the exercise of control and the enjoyment of the fruits of power are—where available—a cardinal good. The very old tend to look backward and to gear their future-oriented arrangements to the *après nous* of their posterity. The temporal transit through life's journey is associated with constantly changing views of prospects and possibilities.

These different outlooks indicate that we think of a lifetime not only as an extent of temporal duration, but also as a succession of definite stages that we must, unless prematurely removed, pass through—each in our own way. We view life not just in terms of a life *span*, but in terms of a life *cycle*. From hoary antiquity onward, literary tradition construes this in terms of the seasons of a year, analogizing childhood to spring, youth to summer, maturity to autumn, and old age to winter. Medieval society, habituated more to the diurnal ritual of the ecclesiastical day than to the agrarian cycle of the year, preferred a different analogy: the morning of childhood and youth, the midday of maturity, the evening of old age, and the coming of the eternal night where no man can work. This set a theme to which the "Book of Hours" gave endless variations.

As shown in Table 1, the ancient Romans viewed these stages as a five-part sequence based on functional capacities. The infant has not yet achieved the age of reason, where rational sua-

TABLE 1
Roman Age Periodization

Classification	Age	Notes
Infans (infant)	0–7	Until the shedding of the "milk teeth"
Puer or *puella* (child)	7–12 or 14	Until "marriageable" age, 12 for females, 14 for males
Iuvenis or *junior* (young person)	15–44	The "prime of life," divided into two groups based on legal adulthood. Legal minors (15–24) were too young to serve as judge (*iudex*) or (lowest) magistrate (*quaestor*) and to enter into contracts
Senior (elderly person)	45–59	
Senex (old person)	60 onward	

sion replaces peremptory command. Childhood proper ends at puberty, when one is physically and/or legally able to bear or father children. One then continues as a young adult until such time as one can no longer adequately serve one's prime social function, with men being too old to fight effectively as soldiers, with women being too old to bear children.

The "flourishing age" of classical antiquity, the *akmē* or *floruit* (of ca. age 40) stands as the midway peak of the period between birth and life's ultimate limit of around 80. The dictum that "life begins at 40" gets it exactly wrong. As the Romans saw it, this age represents the "turning point" of one's human flourishing, after which we "go downhill." (Note that the hill-climbing analogy, like the analogy of the seasons, is of the hoariest antiquity and has been the subject of a substantial iconography.)

When we compare this classical Roman periodization with the current American scheme (Table 2), we find much greater complexity in our modern system of age classification. Note first the relatively recent contraction of infancy to the period of babyhood (in England, "infant schools" still go through to the age of 7), second the postponement of the start of adulthood from around 15 to 18/21, and third the postponement of old age from around 60 to around 70. Moreover, the very old represent a relative innovation as a distinct category, reflecting the increase in life expectancy. In English we still lack a distinctive word (counterpart to the German *ein Greis*) to characterize these "survivors

TABLE 2

Contemporary American Age Periodization

Classification	Age		Notes
Baby (infant)	0–2		
Child	3–12		
Preschool age (preliterate)		3–5	
School age (literate)		5–12	
Teenager (adolescent)	13–17		
Young adult	18–24		Legal majority commences for some purposes at 18, for others at 21
Mature adult	25–34		
The middle-aged	35–54		
Early middle years		35–44	
Late middle years		45–54	"Past one's prime" for men, post-menopause for women
Senior citizens			
The elderly	55–69		Recently up from 50
The old	70–79		Recently up from 65
The very old	80 onward		Recently up from 70

of their generation" not just as old, but as *very* old, as "(really) aged." ("Senile" will hardly do, senility being a matter of physical condition—physical and mental infirmity and loss of control—and not of age as such. Some writers nowadays use the awkward "old-old.")[2]

The Rationale of Human Age-Periodication: Phase Transitions

When we contemplate the major descriptive classifications of people by such factors as race, sex, language/culture, and age, we come to realize that not only is a person's age the only description that standardly undergoes change, but that this process is actually inevitable. Everyone who is not prematurely carried off by death is involved in an inescapable transit through the successive stages of life.

[2]The books on aging are nowadays almost beyond counting. One of the best overall surveys I have encountered is Jan and C. Davis Hendricks, *Aging in a Mass Society*, 2d ed. (Cambridge, Mass., 1981).

Age classification proceeds in terms of a series of developmental stages, demarcated by "phase transitions" that represent "milestones" in human development: capacity for speed (around 1–2), capacity for reproduction/biological adulthood (around 10–13), capacity for self-arrangement/social adulthood (around 18–21), onset of marked physical decline (around 55). Observe, however, the inherent variability of these phase transitions. In modern times, the age of adulthood has been postponed. Functional adulthood tends to reflect social needs. It is one thing in a society dedicated to fighting and farming and something different in a technological society. Moreover, as the life expectancy of those who reach adulthood increases, the age at which (in a statistical sense) "people ought to be dead" is also postponed. In ancient times it was perhaps 50 years (despite the Bible's "three score and ten"), nowadays it is perhaps 80. With the progress of nutrition, public health, preventive medicine, and medical breakthroughs it may someday be 90 and perhaps even 100.

The Diversity of Age

These considerations point toward the complexity at issue in age periodization. Strictly speaking, there is not just one age but many ages. For above and beyond the chronological age represented by the length of a person's existence in "real time," there are several very different sorts of ages, as illustrated in Table 3.

Psychological age is particularly interesting in its variability. It reflects the difference between subjective and objective in a manner analogous to the difference between phenomenal (or experienced) and real (or physical) time. The idea that the watched pot never boils, while, on the other hand, time flies when you're having fun, is something familiar from everyday experience. A similar story holds for the difference between the person who is one of the world's hardy perennials and the person aged prematurely in the harsh school of bitter experiences.

Cognitive age affords an interesting instance in how radically age measures can differ from strict chronology. For there clearly is a crucial difference between one's *chronological* life (in terms of mere years) and one's *cognitive* life (in terms of experience and learning), the latter being measured essentially in terms of the *logarithm of the former*. Experience, after all, is cumulative, and

TABLE 3

Different Sorts of "Ages"

Type of age	Description
Psychological age	Determined by how old one "feels" oneself to be. (This is clearly a matter of health, attitude, and outlook. Some people are "old before their time.")
Social age	Determined by social and especially familial role: marriage, children, grandchildren
Cognition age	Determined by progress in the acquisition of information
Physiological age	Determined by bio-medical considerations
Legal age	Defined by context: school starting and ending; eligibility for drinking, driving, voting, military service; retirement and Social Security; etc.
Performance-oriented age	Determined by the sequence novice, learner, competent practitioner, master. (In tournament tennis one is in one's prime in the mid-20's and old at 35.)
Organizational age	Defined as "new fellow" vs. "old timer" (who may be relatively young in years)

each new installment can only add its merely marginal increment of new lessons to the great body of what has gone before.[3] The resulting picture is set out in Table 4. At this reckoning, someone who dies at around 50 has lived only some two-thirds of his expected *chronological* life, but has lived almost 90 percent of his expected *cognitive* life.

Performance-oriented age is chronologically variable in a different sort of way. Old for an athlete may be young for a phi-

---

[3] Thus fresh experience adds its increment dv to the preexisting total v in such a way that its effective import is measured by the proportion dv/v. And $dv/v = \log v$. On such an approach, an increment to one's lifetime has a *cognitive* value determined on strict analogy with Daniel Bernoulli's famous proposal to measure the *economic* value of incremental resources by means of a logarithmic yardstick. (To be sure, man does not live by cognition alone, and many other factors must doubtless enter into an overall assessment.) Initially, I deemed myself to have discovered the principle of the merely logarithmic growth of knowledge through experience. In fact, however, the sagacious Edward Gibbon anticipated it in his *Memoirs of My Life* (London, 1814), p. 187. "The proportion of a part to the whole is the only standard by which we can measure the length of our existence. At the age of twenty, one year is a tenth perhaps of the time which has elapsed within our consciousness and memory: at the age of fifty it is no more than a fortieth, and this relative value continues to decrease till the last sands are shaken out by the hand of death."

TABLE 4

Cognitive vs. Chronological Age

(*Assumed 80-year lifespan*)

Chronological age	Log (age)	Log (age) as percent of log 80	Cognitive age
5	0.70	37%	30
10	1.00	53	42
20	1.30	68	54
30	1.48	78	62
40	1.60	84	67
50	1.70	89	71
60	1.78	94	75
70	1.85	97	78
80	1.90	100	80

losopher. Functional adulthood arrives at 17–18 in a society of soldiers or farmers, but not until around 25–30 in a society of scholars or highly trained professionals. The president of the United States must by law be over 35 but in practice is almost invariably over 45. The president of a university is almost always over 45. The American ambassador to a major European power is seldom under 50. The chief of staff of the U.S. Army, the chief of Naval Operations, and the justices of the Supreme Court are almost always over 55. The Roman virtue of *gravitas* (a mixture of "weight" and "seniority") is a near-inescapable requisite of organizational power. Historically, Western "organization man" has seen maturity as no less powerful a requisite for high office than masculinity. (It is no accident that the chief executive in many an organization is known as "the old man.")

Modern societies see age as a special factor whose bearing is more significant and far-reaching than any other. In developed countries, law and public policy nowadays make a sharper differentiation in regard to age than in regard to sex. The legal disabilities of minors (e.g., their disenfranchisement in the election process) or the special entitlements of the old (in matters of pension or access to social services) set age groupings that override any other sociological grouping by sex, race, religion, etc. Statistical variation hardly justifies such a categorical use of age numbers; we do so in practice only as a matter of administrative convenience. Other categories that are sensitive to more meaningful individual differences are too complex and costly to implement and administer—and would lead us into endless disputes (when does a person attain the "age of discretion" for competency in contractual matters?).

The Conventionality of Phase Transition

It is a most important point in the present context that the phase transitions at work in an age periodization depend on people's judgments of importance—their assessment of "what really matters." And this, clearly, is a fundamentally *evaluative* issue. We position phenomena in a classificatory and descriptive framework whose design involves judgments of importance and significance—value judgments, in short.

A person's position in an age-periodization scheme is not so much an individually descriptive characteristic as a *social* fact with respect to what people deem to be important. Age characterization is in substantial measure not a matter of what one is, but of how one is seen to be—of one's fit into a convention-established category. We are categorized as "young" or "old" less because of what we are or can do as individuals than because people (ourselves doubtless included) think of our age group in a certain way—because the society operates an evaluatively based convention of classification that assigns to people a certain social status or category.

A person's chronological age—together with his or her capacities and capabilities—is a straightforward matter of objective fact. But one's characterization in terms of a descriptive periodization like "a mere child" or "a young woman" or "an old man" reflects a placement in a taxonomic framework whose divisions—those crucial phase transitions that separate one category from the next—are essentially evaluative judgments reflecting certain interests or concerns that we ourselves chose to bring on the scene.

The law fixes a series of age milestones: age of consent, driving age, drinking age, voting age, age of legal majority, retirement age, revocation age (e.g., for driver's or aircraft pilot's licenses). All of these involve a legal fiction of sorts. All impose a sharp division on extremely variable phenomena. Legal age periodization is always something fixed and therefore artificial.

With its hard-and-fast boundaries, it is altogether different from physiological age, which is highly variable. Think for example, of such biomedical milestones as the ability to walk, the acquisition of speech, the loss of milk teeth, puberty, and the attaining of full growth. Think too of the great variability of psychological aging, and the rejuvenating effect of new challenges exemplified by such prominent names as MacArthur, DeGaulle, Adenauer, and Reagan. Any public policy that treats people in terms of age categories ("over 70") rather than in terms of natural groupings ("physically or mentally incapacitated") is inherently problematic. It wears on its very brow the stigma of presumptive inadequacy—a presumption that can be defended only by a substantial advantage in administrative economy.

Age as we talk about it in other, less formalized contexts is something very different—and far less rigid. The periodization of age into successive stages or phases is largely a matter of *social convention*. Actual physical age (in years, days, hours, minutes) is something that is (1) objective and (2) informatively detailed (and thus, potentially, infinitely varied). That's just how the real world is—thought-independent and fine-grainedly concrete. But the age characterizations used in our humanly devised age taxonomies always involve artificial breaks and discontinuities. They reflect rules of thumb designed to render the variety and complexity of the real world amenable to our descriptive convenience. They take the stance that the complexity of real-world detail can be discounted because it just is not important enough to matter in the context of present purpose.

Age periodization, accordingly, is a matter of superimposing certain conventionalized standards of importance on the fundamental objective facts about age and aging. Take the boundary between childhood and adulthood. One leaves childhood when one can begin to function as a full-fledged member of the community, able to do such things as (1) have children (ca. 13 years); (2) bear arms (ca. 15); (3) hold down a job or manage a household (ca. 18); and (4) practice a skilled craft (say goldsmithing) or a profession (say law or medicine)—or, again, play one's role in the realm of business affairs (ca. 21). Different resolutions are made by different cultures in different circumstances. Once you settle that *those* indeed are the "milestones"—that they indeed are what is important and significant—the rest is simply factual (descriptive and "purely informative"). But the fundamental issue of where the milestones fall is evaluative—reflecting a judgment about what "really matters" (is significant, interesting, germane to the fabric of our purposes).

To be sure, in invoking values here we must heed a crucial distinction. The thing at issue is not the value of youth or old age per se. Whether one reveres the old or despises them is beside the point. The crux is the prior issue of a differentiation between youth and middle age and old age, of our deciding that certain milestones—certain rites of passage—are so important in our understanding of what life is all about that they merit adoption as the boundary markers of an age-periodization scheme.

In sum, classifying someone in terms of an age periodization of the usual sort is a step that superimposes value judgments on strictly objective age-related facts. And those evaluations that underlie age periodization reflect social circumstances. This is clearly illustrated by the rise of industrial technology, with its concomitant departure from agrarian patterns of life. The need for more education and training serves to advance the age when adulthood begins. And in a postindustrial society based on the primacy of tasks that require substantial professional training, the age of adulthood advances even more. Still, specific leadership roles apart, we tend to value age as such rather less than people used to do. In the West, at least, we do not venerate the aged for their own sake, as the Chinese and Japanese, for example, do. And for good reason. The primary advantage of age over youth lies in the domain of experience. But experience is always experience of the past, and in a situation of change and innovation, the past tends to be irrelevant to the present. It is primarily in situations of social stability that age is of positive advantage, because the teachings of experience have ongoing relevance.

Thought Experiments

The attunement of age periodization to matters of evaluation is brought home to us particularly clearly when we engage in thought experimentation by projecting hypotheses that radically alter the character of the group whose values will be relevant. For example, consider how this matter of age would appear if people had a life expectancy very different from ours—one of 20 years, say, or of 200.[4] We can consider in only the most speculative way how they would then revise their periodization of life. Their circumstances would change so radically that value changes would be bound to follow. Age categorization is fact-based—geared to the way people see the course of nature as they experience it. And this involves a lot of specifics that mere hypotheses tend to leave out of account.

For example, very little is accomplished by the mere supposition that the half-life, average-age midpoint of human beings increases from roughly 40 to roughly 450 years. For one thing, we would have to know at what point of the life cycle those extra years are to come. Are we dealing with a very prolonged infancy, where it takes 800 years to get people where we presently have them at age 2? Are we to look at them as aging to 80 at more or less the present rate, and then frozen into an interminable period of glacial decreptitude and decline. Or are they to gain all those extra years by taking 800 years to cover the developmental period currently traversed in the decade from 40 to 50?

If the latter, how tragic for the practitioners of professions like tennis—or, if common report is right, creative theoretical mathematics or physics—where most contributors have their best work behind them by the age of 30 and are "over the hill" at 35. But perhaps how much worse yet for humanists—historians, say, or philosophers. What prospects are there for fledgling assistant professors, with a flourishing Leibniz on hand to put in another good 500 years of service and Kant as a mere lad with 600 years to go? Where will those classicists be on whom Bentley has a head start of 300 years and who would have to labor for centuries under the censorious glance of von Wilamowitz-Moellendorf? Or what of the historians who would have to compete with a Leopold von Ranke who has a 100 years head start and still has almost 800 years to go?

So the details will matter a great deal. For example, how we would think about the role of age in a society of Methusalahs would clearly depend a good deal on the economic and professional structure of the society—on how important a role youth-

---

[4]See, in this connection, Kenneth Boulding's splendid essay "The Menace of Methusalah," *Journal of the Washington Academy of Science* (Oct. 1965).

ful vigor has in the requirements of the group. If preindustrial warfare were important in a society in which only 1 percent of the population was in the years of fighting trim, "able-bodiedness" would doubtless emerge as a factor of much importance and respect.

The Role of Values

The moral of the age-periodization story thus lies in the fundamental role of values. Appearances to the contrary notwithstanding, when one calls a person, *young* or *old* or *middle-aged*, one is not simply making a statement of descriptive fact—but is obliquely making value judgments as well. An age-periodization scheme is not just (not simply or merely) a *descriptive* mechanism. In its placement of boundary markers between successive stages, it reflects and embodies a commitment to evaluations in the area of interest, significance, importance. It is predicated on accepting the idea that the *really important* (significant, crucial) phase transitions in the development of a human life are those that it incorporates. And as such it can be appropriate or inappropriate, sensible or silly. Moreover, given the plausible principle that to *use* a scheme is to *endorse* it, we do, in characterizing someone in terms of such a scheme, de facto endorse the evaluations that underlie it. Employing a given age-periodization scheme reflects a certain *ideology*—a way of looking at the world that reflects our "subjective" views every bit as much as the objective nature of what we see.

The philosophers of ancient Greece liked to pose the question of whether certain facts obtained "by nature" (*phusē*$_i$) or merely "by (human) convention" (*nomē*$_i$). When someone is categorized by an age classification such as "middle-aged," we have little alternative but to hedge by saying that this obtains *by both*, seeing that the issue is one of conventionalized human evaluations grafted onto a natural state of affairs. For better or worse, an age-periodization scheme is predicated on a certain vision of the good life—and almost inevitably one that can, by its very nature, be called into question.[5]

[5] This essay draws on the author's discussion of "Life's Seasons," in *Forbidden Knowledge* (Dordrecht, 1987).

Gender Issues

THE BOOK of *Genesis* informs us that woman was created as a *companion* to man. This of course leaves quite unexplained why the duality of sexes also extends to the far less sociable sectors of the organic domain. But it does at any rate emphasize clearly that, with respect to the human community, the existence of two sexes possesses an importance that transcends the requirements of procreation and the perpetuation of the race.

The intimately familial (rather than more diffusely tribal) organization of society, with its powerful impetus to provision for the future, would be crucially undermined in a unisexual community of intelligent creatures. And this in turn would gravely impair the development of civilization and all its works. Concern for our heritage and concern for our posterity are inextricably intertwined.

The partition of our species into males and females obviously has the most far-reaching significance for the way in which people conduct their everyday lives. Once we know that a *person* is at issue, a priority-ordered series of questions immediately arises:

1. Is it a human being (rather than a person of some alien species)? (We generally take an affirmative answer for granted.)
2. Is it a normal human or a "monster" of some sort—a Siamese twin, a creature with two heads, etc.? (Again, we generally take an affirmative answer for granted.)
3. What is the person's sex?

4. What is the person's age or age group?
5. What is the person's society (culture, language)?

Only thereafter do we branch out into the more specialized questions of race, occupation, marital status, etc. As this prioritizing indicates, once we know that a normal human being is at issue, the matter of gender rises to the top of the agenda for us—a fact that is straightforwardly reflected in those Indo-European languages that prominently separate things into the masculine and the feminine.

The importance of sex as a formative force in human affairs scarcely needs emphasis in this era of post-Freudian sensibilities. On the contrary, we perhaps need to recognize that it has been exaggerated. Work, parenting, entertaining, sports, and communality with friends and relatives each occupy most of us to a greater extent than making love or war with selected members of the opposite sex. Sleep, work, preparing and eating food, taking in information from reading matter or television, and other such gender-indifferent preoccupations each figure more prominently in the time budget of most adults than do matters of gender-specific activities in courting and coupling.

Still, matters relating to gender are clearly of major importance in our lives. Why, then, have philosophers generally taken so little notice of them? The best explanation seems to be that philosophers have traditionally wanted to focus on the human condition at large—on those issues that affect *all* human beings. And while being male-or-female pertains to all of us as part of our humanity, being specifically male or specifically female does not. After all, the circumstance that one is a male or a female is a matter of mere contingency, a mere happenstance of one's biology, an "accident" in the Aristotelian terminology of traditional philosophy. Unlike our rationality, it is not an essential feature of our humanity. Feminist critics to the contrary notwithstanding, classical philosophers do not worship maleness and tacitly presuppose that the only people worth discussing are males; they ignore gender and treat mere differences of sex as unworthy of notice. It is a just and proper appreciation of the fact that humanity as such is what matters, and mere maleness or femaleness is something incidental, that has led traditional philosophers to take the line they do.

There is, however, another noteworthy aspect of the matter—

namely, the fundamentally intellectualist bias of classical philosophy. What traditional philosophy mainly cares about is the matter of our mental capabilities. (From its standpoint we are *Homo sapiens*: "Man is the *rational* animal," say the ancient Aristotelians; "I am because I think," say the modern Cartesians.) And so, the classical philosophers thought what is crucial about us is our mental capacities; sex, like hair color or skin pigmentation, is a mere incidental. The intellectualist bias led classical philosophers to consign our sexuality to the level of mere incidentals. But while the philosophers of earlier eras rightly saw that being male or female is not all-important, they wrongly thought that the matter was not important enough to deserve philosophical recognition. When they thought about women explicitly as such, classical philosophers simply reflected the stereotypes of their time and place. In fact, considering how little traditional philosophical deliberations at the level of theory would justify any sort of aspersions on women, their treatment in practice at the pens of the philosophers of the past is both irrational and disgraceful.

On their own principles, philosophers should see people as rational beings first, as human beings second, and as men and women a distant third. After all, exactly how substantial is the role of gender-based concerns in human affairs? Only for some people—be they theoreticians (Freud, Havelock Ellis), academic voyeurs (Masters and Johnson), publicists ("Dr. Ruth"), or practitioners (Don Juan, Casanova, Fanny Hill)—does sex feature as the number one item among life's priorities. Most people place their priorities (or obsessions) elsewhere—money, power, health, sports, mountaineering, drink, or whatever. The hardest thing for philosophers—as for most individual human beings— is to get the mix right, to design a rational economy of attention and preoccupation that gets a sensible sort of balance between various human needs and wants.

Two things are obvious here. One is that without plausible investment of time and attention in the sexual dimension of human existence, we can neither achieve a full life for ourselves nor ensure a continuing future for our species. The other is that if one goes too far in this direction—if sexual concerns are too high on the scale of priorities in one's agenda of life—then one is no longer the sort of person with whom it is possible for people to live on a comfortable footing, oneself included.

And so, despite its manifest shortcomings and deficiencies, there is an important element of truth in the traditional philosopher's emphasis on the fact that we humans are (potentially) rational, moral, and social creatures. Among our most important and characteristic features as members of the species *Homo sapiens* are our possession of reason (intelligence); our role as moral agents who can act for the right or the wrong; and our social nature as members of a wider community (fellow citizens interacting within a framework of rules). In all three regards, men and women stand on exactly the same footing. In point of intelligence, in their capacity to do right or wrong, and in their standing before the law (be it human or divine), men and women are—or should be—altogether equal. Insofar as philosophical deliberations should put first things first, the *practical* importance of our differentiation into men and women is ultimately not matched by an equivalent theoretical importance. For with regard to that fundamental issue of our status as human beings and its immediate implications, men and women stand on wholly equivalent ground.

In particular, morality cuts across the sexual divide—the imperative to moral agency bears with equal weight on men and women alike. To be sure, there is no way of being a good person except by doing so in two rather different ways—being a good man or being a good woman. But the general *principles* involved are exactly the same either way.

But is it really true that men and women are on exactly the same footing from the moral point of view? Are gender-connected differences really irrelevant in this regard?

Well . . . yes and no. Consider an analogy. Do physically strong and powerful people not have a "special moral responsibility" to take particular care with others in physical interactions (handshakes, backslaps, jostling in crowds, etc.)? Of course they do. But this "special moral responsibility" is merely a particular application to their specific situation of an overreaching universal moral principle: "Don't injure others through heedless carelessness!" And so with men and women. No doubt their particular condition puts them into a characteristic relationship with others. (A man, for example, cannot—as things stand—have the special moral commitment toward a womb-borne protoperson.) But these sex-differential moral relations are always matters of the particular application of universal principles to special cases: "Exercise appropriate concern of the welfare and well-being of your incipient progeny" holds as much for men as for women; the *general* principles involved in protecting one's offspring are exactly the same on both sides. From this perspective—that of the basic principles of human concern—men and women do indeed start on exactly the same universal footing. The overall significance of gender issues is uncontestable, but their specifically *moral* relevancy is very much in doubt.

SEVEN

Evolution and Intelligence

Why Are We So Smart?

Why are we humans so smart? How is it that we possess the intellectual talent to create mathematics, medicine, science, engineering, architecture, literature, and other comparably splendid intellectual disciplines? What explains the immense power of our cognitive capacities?

The *general* direction—at any rate—of the answer to this query about human intelligence is relatively straightforward. Basically, we are so smart because that is our place in evolution's scheme of things. Different sorts of creatures have different ecological niches, different specialities that enable them to find their evolutionary way down the corridor of time. Some are highly prolific, some physically tough, some swift of foot, some hard to spot, some extremely shy. *Homo sapiens* is different. For the evolutionary instrument of our species is *intelligence*—with everything that this involves in the way of abilities and versatilities.

And, of course, it is not all just a matter of luck—of fate's lottery bringing intelligence our way. Evolution's bio-engineering is the crucial factor. Bees and termites can achieve impressive prodigies of collective effort. But an insect developed under the aegis of evolution could not become as smart as a man because the information-processing needs of the lifestyle opportunities afforded by its physical endowment are too modest to push it to the development of intelligence.

Smarts are an inherent concomitant of our physical endowment. Our bodies have many more independently movable parts (more "degrees of freedom") than those of most other creatures.[1] And this circumstance has significant implications. Suppose a system with n switches, each capable of assuming an ON or OFF position. Then there are 2 exp n states in which the system can find itself. With $n = 3$ there are only 8 system-states, but with n doubling to 6 there are already 64 states. As a body grows more complex and its configuration takes on more degrees of freedom, the range of alternative possible states expands rapidly (exponentially). Merely keeping track of its actual position is difficult enough. To plan ahead is more difficult still. If there are m possible states that the system can assume now, then when it comes to selecting its next position, there are also m choices, and for the next two there are $m \times m$ alternatives overall (ignoring unrealizable combinations). So with a two-step planning horizon, the 3-state system has 64 alternatives, while the 6-state system has 4,096. With a mere doubling of states, the planning problem has become complicated by a factor of 64.

The degrees of freedom inherent in variable movement over time are pivotal factors here. The moment one walks upright and begins to develop the modes of motion that this new posture facilitates—creeping, running, leaping, etc.—one has many more problems of physical management to solve.

Considerations of this sort make it evident that a vertebrate having a more highly articulated skeleton, with many independently operable bones and bone complexes, faces vastly greater difficulties in management and manipulation—in what military jargon calls "command and control." Physically more versatile animals have to be smarter simply because they are physically more versatile.

We humans are driven to ever-greater capabilities in information acquisition and management by the greater demands of the lifestyle of our ecological niche. The complexity of our sophisticated surveillance mechanisms in the context of friend-or-foe

---

[1] The human skeleton has some 220 bones, about the same number as a cat when tail bones are excluded. A small monkey has around 120. Of course, what matters for present purposes is *independently* moving parts. This demotes "thousand leggers" and—thanks to fingers, among other things—takes us out of the cat's league.

identification is an illustration. We can observe at a considerable distance that people are looking at us, discriminating minute differences in eye orientation in this context. The development of our senses, with our ability to discriminate odors, colors, and sounds, is another example. Environmental surveillance is crucial for our lifestyle. We have to know which features of our environment we must heed and which can safely be ignored. The handling of such a volume of information calls for selectivity and for sophisticated processing mechanisms—for intelligence in short. Not only must our bodies be the right size to support our physical operations and activities, but our brains must be the right size as well.

The complexities of information management and control pose unrelenting evolutionary demands. To process a large volume of information, nature must fit us out with a large brain. A battleship needs more elaborate mechanisms for guidance and governance than a rowboat. A department store needs a more elaborate managerial apparatus than a corner grocery. To operate a sophisticated body, you need a sophisticated brain. The evolution of the human brain is the story of nature's struggle to provide the machinery of information management and control needed by creatures of increasing physical versatility. A feedback cycle comes into operation—a complex body requires a larger brain for command and control, and sustaining a larger brain requires a larger body, whose operational efficiency in turn places greater demands on that brain for the managerial functions required to provide for survival and the assurance of posterity. As can be illustrated by comparing the brain weights of different mammalian species, the growing complexities and versatilities of animal bodies involve a physical lifestyle whose difficulties of information processing and management require an increasingly powerful brain. How one makes one's living also matters: insect-eating and fruit-eating monkeys have heavier brains, for their size, than leaf-eating ones do.[2]

Here then is the immediate (and rather trivial) answer to our question: we are as intelligent as we are because that is how we

[2] At any given time in evolutionary history, the then-current herbivores tended to have smaller brains than the contemporary carnivores. Richard Dawkins, *The Blind Watchmaker* (London, 1981), p. 190.

had to evolve to fill our place in nature's scheme of things. We are so smart because evolution's bio-engineering needs to provide the smarts that allow us to achieve and maintain the lifestyle appropriate to our ecological niche. If we were not so intelligent, we would not be here as the creatures we are. We have all those splendid intellectual capacities because we require them in order to be ourselves.

But there remains the problem of why evolution would take this course. Surely we did not need to be *that* smart to outwit the saber-toothed tiger or domesticate the sheep. Let us explore this aspect of the matter a little.

The things we have to do to manage our lifestyle must not only be *possible* for us; they must in general be *easy* for us (so easy that most of them can be done unthinkingly and even unconsciously). If our problem-solving resources were frequently strained to the limit, often groaning under the burden of the problems they are called on by nature to resolve in the interests of our lifestyle, then we just would not have that lifestyle.

For evolution to do its work, the survival problems that creatures confront have to be by and large easy for the mechanisms at their disposal. And this fundamental principle holds just as true for cognitive as for biological evolution. If cognitive problem-solving were too difficult for our mental resources, we would not evolve as problem-solving creatures. If we had to go to as great lengths to work out the sum $2 + 2$ as to extract the cube root of a number, or if it took us as long to discriminate 3-sided figures from 4-sided ones as it takes to discriminate between 296-sided figures and 297-sided ones, then these sorts of issues would simply remain outside our cognitive repertoire. The "average" problems for survival and thriving that are posed by our lifestyle must be of the right level of difficulty for us—that is, they must be rather easy. And that calls for excess capacity. All of the "ordinary" problems of one's mode of life must be solvable quickly in real time—and with enough idle capacity left over to cope with the unusual.

A brain capable of doing all that is needed to sustain the life of a complex and versatile intelligent creature will remain underutilized much of the time. To cope at times of peak demand, it will have a great deal of excess capacity to spare for other issues at slack times. And so, any brain powerful enough to accomplish those occasionally necessary tasks will have the excess capacity at most normal times to pursue various challenging projects that have nothing whatever to do with survival.

These considerations resolve the objection that evolution cannot explain our smarts because we are a lot smarter than evolution demands—that, after all, evolution does not set us examinations on higher mathematics or theoretical physics. The point is not that such disciplines somehow afford humans with an evolutionary advantage, but rather, that the capacities and abilities that make these enterprises possible are evolutionarily advantageous. That evolution equips us with a reserve capacity that makes these activities possible is a side benefit. An intelligent creature whose capacities do not allow development in these directions just is not smart enough to pass evolution's examinations in other matters, and so would not be able to make intelligence its evolutionary specialty after all.

The brain/computer analogy once again proves helpful in this connection. Very different things can be at stake with being "simple": the simplicity of "hardware" at issue with comparatively uncomplex *computers* is one sort of thing, and the simplicity of "software" at issue with comparatively uncomplex *programs* is something quite different. And there are clearly trade-offs here. Solving problems of the same level of difficulty is generally more easily accomplished on a more sophisticated (more complex) computing machine. Something of an inverse relationship obtains: greater machine complication can make the actual use of the machine easier and less demanding. It is generally easier to program more "advanced" (i.e., complex) machines to do various sorts of tasks. And this is exactly our own circumstance, as creatures that make our evolutionary way in the world by intelligence, we require a rather powerful and complicated brain, a brain that enables us also to realize all sorts of impressive but evolution-irrelevant achievements.

To be sure, evolution is not, in general, overgenerous. For example, evolution will not develop creatures whose running speed is vastly greater than what is needed to escape their predators, to catch their prey, or to realize some similarly strictly utilitarian objective. But intelligence and its works are a clear exception to this general rule, owing to its self-catalyzing nature. With *cognitive* capacities, the character of the issues prevents a holding back: once one can do a little with calculation or with infor-mation-processing, one can in principle do a lot. Once evolution lets intelligence in through the door, it gets "the run of the house." When bio-design takes the route of intelligence to se-cure an evolutionary advantage for a creature, it embarks on a slippery slope. Having started along this road, there is no easy and early stop. For once a species embarks on intelligence as its instrument for coping with nature, then the pressure of species-internal competition enters as a kind of hothouse-forcing pro-cess. Intelligence itself becomes a goad to further development simply because intelligence is, as it were, developmentally self-energizing.

The result of these deliberations is straightforward. Intelli-gence is the evolutionary specialty of *Homo sapiens*. If we were markedly less smart than we in fact are, we would not have been able to survive. Or rather, more accurately, we would not have been able to develop into the sort of creatures we have become. Intelligence constitutes the characteristic specialty that provides the competitive advantage that has enabled our species to make its evolutionary way in this world's scheme of things. We are so smart because being smart is necessary for *us* to be here at all.

Why Are We So Dumb?

But at this point a very different question arises, one that points in the exactly opposite direction: why are we not a great deal more intelligent than we are? Why can we not master a for-eign language with a single week's concerted effort or learn cal-culus in a fortnight? What explains our manifest cognitive defi-ciencies and limitations? Why are we so dumb?

This question is also one that can in principle be answered in evolutionary terms.[3] But it has two importantly different aspects:

---

[3] Some may think it is incongruous to ask for an evolutionary explanation for something that has not happened. But the issue is rather one of using basic prin-ciples of natural process to explain why evolution does not take certain routes. In this regard, the situation with respect to intelligence (i.e., *cognitive* agility) is not dissimiliar from that with regard to motion (i.e., *physical* agility). Explaining why evolution has not produced a hyperintelligent mammal is structurally akin to explaining why it has not produced a hyperswift one by outfitting creatures with organic wheels. For an interesting treatment of this issue, see Jared Dia-mond, "The Biology of the Wheel," *Nature*, 302 (Apr. 14, 1983): 572–73.

(1) why are we not *comprehensively* smarter by way of enhanced mind-power for the species as a whole, and (2) why are we not *statistically* smarter by way of an increase in the relative proportion of smart people within the presently constituted range of intelligence levels. Let us consider these issues one at a time.

First off, to be a substantially smarter species we would need a much bigger brain. To manage this on prevailing bio-engineering principles would require a larger—less agile—body, forcing us to forgo the advantages of maneuverability and versatility. To process twice the information would require a brain roughly four times its present size. But to quadruple our brain weight, we would need a body sixteen times its present weight.[4] A body of so great a weight not only is extremely cumbersome but also involves enormous demands for energy. The most plausible and probable move would then be to opt for a very different ecological niche and take to the water, joining our mammalian cousins the whales and dolphins. The intellectually stimulating surroundings of a land environment, with its invitations to technological development and record-keeping, would all be denied us. That gain in brain power would have come at an awesome cost, the sacrifice of the collective intelligence of the social institutionalization of tool-using creatures. The price is one that an evolutionary development of intelligence cannot afford.[5]

There remains, however, the question of why we humans should not be smarter by way of a statistical improvement in the relative proportion of very smart people in our existing species? With this shift of questions, we now move from the issue of bio-engineering a "more intelligent" *species* to the development of a "more intelligent" *population*—one in which the percentage of people qualifying as "superior" in intelligence by the prevailing standards would be substantially enlarged.

[4] On this issue compare J. B. S. Haldane's insightful and provocative essay "On Being the Right Size," in his collection *Possible Worlds and Other Papers* (New York, 1928).

[5] Of course here—as elsewhere—we cannot let matters rest with speaking of an evolutionary process in this rather anthropomorphic way. In the final analysis, we have to cash in these metaphors in terms of different groups (tribes, clans) of humanoids chancing to produce a bumper crop of more than ordinarily intelligent individuals and finding themselves at a reproductive disadvantage thereby because of their comparatively greater risk-aversiveness. But no imaginative student of recent demographic phenomena will find difficulty in envisioning an appropriate sort of scenario here.

It is here that the social dimension of the matter comes into prominence. Consider the following sort of case. You and I interact in a competitive situation of potential benefit that has a roughly zero-sum character, with one party's gain as the other's loss. Two alternatives are open to us: to COLLABORATE with each other or to try to OUTWIT each other. If we collaborate, we will share the resultant benefit (say, by each getting one-half of it). If we compete, then the winner takes all; whoever succeeds gains the whole benefit. The overall situation thus stands as depicted in Table 5.

If I see my chances of winning to be given by the probability p, then my expectations stand as follows:

EV (collaborate) $= p(0.5\ B) + (1 - p)(0.5\ B) = 0.5\ B$
EV (compete) $= p(B) + (1 - p)(0) = pB$

As long as p is less than one-half, that is, as long as my subjectively appraised chances of winning are less than even, collaboration is the sensible course relative to the balance of expectations. But when p exceeds one-half, the balance moves in favor of noncooperation. If one views the benefits of self-reliance optimistically, then rationality inclines against cooperation; it favors going one's own competitive way and "taking one's chances." Thus people who see themselves as comparatively more clever are less likely to collaborate. And a society in which this state prevails pays the price of a weakened impetus to cooperative effort.

To picture the structure of the situation more graphically, consider the state of affairs reflected in the (purely hypothetical) statistical distributions presented in Table 6. If we suppose that people interact randomly, then in Case I well over half (54 percent) of pairwise interpersonal interactions are between cognitive compeers (equals), compared with well under one-half (46 percent) in Case II. Given that it takes two to cooperate, the upshot is that the majoritarian social norm would provide a rational impetus for cooperation in Case I but would encourage competition in Case II.

Accordingly, if we humans were statistically more intelligent than we are, the greater success of our interactions with nature would doubtless incline us toward a still-higher estimation of our intellectual powers, but, in consequence, in many of us, the

TABLE 5

Hypothetical Pay-Offs in a Two-Way Competition

Alternative	Fortune favors me	Fortune favors you
We collaborate	0.5 B / 0.5 B	0.5 B / 0.5 B
We fail to collaborate	B / 0	0 / B

NOTE: B = benefit. A table entry of the form *x/y* represents the gains for the two parties, *x* for me and *y* for you, respectively.

TABLE 6

Hypothetical Distribution of Cognitive Ability Before and After Improvement

(*Percent*)

Case	Highly able	Moderately able	Substandardly able
I. Current distribution (hypothetical)	10%	70%	20%
II. Distribution after improvement	30%	60%	10%

NOTE: The ability levels are to be taken as fixed by the prevailing standards.

impetus to a collectively beneficial collaboration with others would become undermined. A statistical improvement in cognitive ability would tend to increase the number of people who, trusting to their intelligence, would try to outwit others instead of "playing by the rules"—which, after all, are largely designed to protect the nonadvantaged. The natural outrage we feel, even as children, against noncooperation and our rational animus toward those who do not play fair are patently connected in the evolutionary order with the fact that most of us draw substantial benefits from a system in which people "play by the rules." In a way, statistical inferiority serves as an equalizer. The darkness of general incomprehension creates a smoky battlefield where parties of different levels of ability can contend on a much more even footing. The social cooperation conducive to human well-being overall benefits from a suitable admixture of incapacity.

As the bee illustrates, the evolution of cooperation certainly does not require individual intelligence. Quite to the contrary. As the number of "clever" people who pride themselves on their strength of intellect increases, social cohesion becomes more difficult to obtain. University faculties are notoriously difficult to manage. Experts are thorns in the sides of popes and presidents alike. No sect manages to keep on easy terms with its theologians. (Anyone who is familiar with the ways of an intellectual avant garde such as the Bloomsbury circle has some idea of the difficulties of socializing people who see themselves as more than ordinarily clever.) It is easy to envision how in numerous circumstances intelligence militates against cooperation.

We humans require intelligence to structure our interactions with nature into generally beneficial channels. But no less importantly, we are collectively so situated that we need to cooperate and collaborate with one another in ways that conduce to the general benefit. And if we were, on statistical balance, more intelligent than we are, such cooperation and collaboration would be more difficult to achieve. People would become more reliant on their own wits and retreat from reliance on others, deeming themselves "above the common herd."

To some extent, then, dumbness is evolutionarily advantageous. For an individual's prospects of surviving and thriving are generally bound up with how well or ill things are going in the society of which that individual is part (as wars and economic depressions indicate). And insofar as a society's well-being can be undermined by a *surfeit* of intelligent individuals, evolution will (obliquely) select against individual intelligence.

The interesting and perhaps surprising lesson thus emerges that if we humans were—on balance—to become substantially more intelligent than we actually are, then the rational impetus to socialization and interpersonal cooperation would be undermined. If people were *bodily* stronger than they are, they would have to be larger and heavier—and would thus be hampered physically by the resultant cumbersomeness. If people were *mentally* stronger than they are, they would be hampered socially by a resultant impetus toward trying to outwit one another. The prospect of effective socialization in the service of communal interests and the general good would be diminished. And any such result would clearly be evolutionarily counterproductive. One very good reason why we are not a lot smarter is just that it would not be a very smart move for us to be so.

These deliberations yield the odd-sounding lesson that evolutionary pressure is a two-edged sword that can cut in opposite directions as regards the development of intelligence. Evolution is a process in which the balance of cost and benefit is constantly maintained in a delicate equilibrium. And this general phenomenon is vividly illustrated in the·particular case of our cognitive capacities. On the one hand, we humans are not less intelligent than we are because if we were, we would incur an evolutionary disadvantage in our *physical* dealings with nature. But analogously, we are not more intelligent than we are, because if we were, we would *also* suffer an evolutionary disability by becoming disadvantaged in our *social* dealings with one another, since this would weaken the impetus to cooperation. In its handling of intelligence, evolution, like a shrewd gambler, is clever enough to follow the precept "Quit while you're ahead."

EIGHT

Limits and Limitations

HUMAN BEINGS are creatures of needs and wants. And we have more of them than we can ever possibly manage to satisfy. An inescapable inability to obtain all of the things we would like to have marks us as limited and rather powerless. It is, to be sure, imaginable that otherwise intelligent creatures inserted into nature by evolutionary processes might be wholly unaware of their needs (which are "automatically" met in their ecological niche), and moreover, be so adjusted as to have no wants over and above those needs. This is, one must suppose, just barely possible. But in our own case it is certainly not the actual state of affairs. We have numerous felt needs and wants, and a good part of our efforts and energies are spent in trying to satisfy them—generally with very limited success.

The Dimensions of Finitude

We do and must conduct our lives under the realization of limits and limitations. From infancy onward, we learn painful lessons of finitude and incapacity. From the moment we enter the world (often to the greeting of a rude slap), we discover that "we cannot have it all our way"—that we cannot satisfy our needs and wants to the extent that we would like. From our earliest days, we learn the lessons of limitedness and powerlessness in the school of bitter experience. The fact that we have desires we cannot afford to fulfill, and talents and interests that we cannot develop with the time, energy, and resources at our disposal, means that life is a constant succession of choices. We are creatures committed to the project of evaluation because we must continually compare and contrast the merits of discordant objectives and prioritize our desiderata.

The principal dimensions of human finitude are time, knowledge, resources, power over ourselves (ability, talent, skill), power over externals, and the capacity to enjoy. Let us briefly consider these various parameters of finitude.

Time. The limits of time are perhaps the most intractable and most intimidating of all the finitudes that confront us. The stark and unwelcome fact of our own mortality is something we must all come to terms with. (Spinoza's contention that the wise never think of death gets the matter backwards; it is only the foolish and heedless who never give their mortality a thought.) There is also the fact that most of the ends we pursue are, even where achievable, not to be realized as quickly as we desire.

Knowledge. There are two main sorts of knowledge, theoretical and practical. And both are available to us on only a limited basis. Practical knowledge guides us in getting our way in the world, on the way to go about things so as to secure health, wealth, happiness, and other goods. But clearly, no matter how much we get we will always want more. Theoretical knowledge involves information acquired for its own sake—purely and simply for alleviating the discomfort of ignorance, of lacking answers to our questions. And here too we always fall short in varying degrees: with every question we answer, the door opens to new ones still to be resolved. These cognitive limitations of ours have far-reaching ramifications. For we are so circumstanced that (1) there are questions we need to answer in conducting our lives through the instrumentality of thought, while nevertheless (2) the information that is securely at our disposal does not suffice to answer these questions with anything approaching certainty. (For example, we need a drink but cannot tell whether yon water, apparently the only available drink, is actually safe and unpolluted.) Even when we reason carefully, we still fall into error. Often we are led by merely *incomplete* information into outright *mistaken* judgments. All too often our vaunted knowledge is not merely deficient but defective.

Resources. We need food, shelter, and clothing. And beyond such necessities, we generally want the myriad goods that money can buy (to postpone for the moment considering those things that it cannot). The acquisition of an ever-enlarging range of "material" goods is a prime desideratum for all too many of us. And quantity alone is not the issue (after all, one can only use so many automobiles or party dresses). The path of their *qualitative* enhancement—newer, larger, better, safer, etc.—stretches almost endlessly before us as a road along which we can never gravel as far as we would ideally like.

Talent, ability, and skill. Some of the most disconcerting limitations we confront are ones that pertain to—of all things—*ourselves*. There are countless things we would like to do—play sports, speak languages, play musical instruments—that we cannot now (or, alas, *ever*) do as well as we would like. All the money in the world cannot buy such capabilities for us, and the most we can do against this is to regard them—in fox-and-grapes fashion—as unimportant.

Power. The capacity to have things one's way—to bend the world's course of events to the twists and turns of one's own desires—is the quintessence of power. It is the ability to impose one's will on other people and on the world at large. Though all of us can achieve something and so much, we remain obviously deficient in this regard. Born in circumstances not of our choosing in a world not of our making, we have no choice but to accept the dictates of fate in this race for power and influence. And viewed in the world's larger scheme of things, the power of even the most powerful of humans is weak and trifling.

Capacity to enjoy. No matter how much we *have*, there is only so much that we can *enjoy*. We can only take pleasure in so much eating, so much entertainment, so much companionship. With most forms of enjoyment, there is soon "too much of a good thing"; we become satiated and yearn for change. Aristotle exempted the pleasures of the mind from this rule, but even that is very dubious as long as we are constituted as we are. As things stand, our capacity to enjoy any one sort of thing—and indeed every sort of thing—is limited, hedged in by habituation, boredom, and the fatigue of satiation. The record suggests that even "people who have everything" do not live lives of great happiness. How rarely are the dreams of adolescence realized in later life—and how frequently hollow are the joys of the few "lucky" ones who manage to realize them.

Insatiability: The Problem of Escalation

Not only are we limited as a species, but there is also the cruel fact of our limitations as individuals. For each of us, there are many things available to some but beyond our own reach. Here, clearly, is a source of vexation—and of envy.

There are many desiderata that we want to have in a comparative rather than absolute way. The desirability of some goods, like money or power, does not inhere simply in their possession as such, but largely consists in having more of them than others have. It lies in the very nature of such goods that we must for the most part fall short of them, since, obviously, it lies in the nature of things that *most* of us cannot possess them to an extent greater than people in general do.

The existence of limits means that one can never obtain as much as one might, in theory, wish to have. But why is this *theoretical* state of affairs so significant? Why should we not become satisfied in *practice*, resting content with what we do have, and not concerning ourselves with that unrealistic prospect of getting ever more? The stark reality, alas, is that this is just not how things work. Human nature decrees otherwise. Like it or not, the cruel and crucial fact about the human condition is that our wants are insatiable.

You are young and poor. A thousand dollars looks to be a fortune to you. By dint of luck or effort you manage to secure it. Are you now satisfied? Not on your life! Suddenly the securing of ten thousand dollars becomes important. Or again—you yearn to see the Eiffel Tower, to sample the sidewalk cafés of the Left Bank, to stroll on the Ile de la Cité in the shade of Notre Dame. Finally you manage to get to Paris and savor the objects of your dreams. Are you now satisfied? Not at all! Suddenly Buckingham Palace, the Houses of Parliament, and the crown jewels of the Tower of London acquire a newfound interest for you. No matter what you master or learn or get, what you have is always only the start. A satisfied want is simply the first step toward others. We are—most of us—caught up in an inexcusable escalation of demands. Our "human nature" is such that the limit of our desires is like a horizon that moves ever onward to remain frustratingly out of reach; once they are actually met, we almost automatically raise our sights to new levels of acquisition and attainment.

This progression of our wants above and beyond the level of attainment is simply a psychological feature of the human condition in its given form. Only rare and unusually self-controlled people can free themselves from the firm grasp of this mechanism of escalation. The rest of us in the great, gray, "normal" majority are caught up in the circumstance that not only are we in fact limited, but the course of events in our lives is such as to keep us painfully ever-mindful of this fact. Not only is *Homo sapiens* a creature of limits, but being constituted as we psychologically are, we cannot—for the most part—avoid being sensitively aware of them. We know full well that we cannot get our own way in this world—that we cannot obtain as much of what we want as we would like. Strive and succeed as we may at acquiring more of the goods of this world, we cannot overcome those structurally inherent limits and limitations.

Reactions to Limits

How is one to respond to the reality of human limitation? Three basic alternatives are possible: *willful ignorance* ("look the other way"); *discouraged defeatism* ("give up the struggle"); and *realistic acceptance* ("make the best of a difficult situation"). Which course is best from the rational point of view?

To begin with, one can simply shut one's eyes to the existence of limits, and, ostrich-like, stick one's head into the sand as far as the entire issue is concerned. Forgetting all about limits and limitations, one can press ahead blindly, ever striving for more and more in a willful ignorance that invites certain frustration in the end. Or again, one can adopt the course of discouraged defeatism. Taking the fox-and-grapes approach, one says to oneself, "I can't have my way—so the whole game's not worth the candle." Failing to compromise with the awkward realities of life, one gives up the struggle and settles for far less than is readily available. But this is hardly the rational approach. That leaves realistic acceptance. Acknowledging the reality of limits and recognizing that one simply cannot get all one desires of the good things of this world, one nevertheless proceeds in the conviction that it is possible to do better than one has managed so far and endeavors to effect improvements in the existing condition of things. One simply struggles along to do the best one can. This third course, though far from ideal, is certainly the most sensible one—the best choice within a hard option. And there is good theoretical justification for this.

There are two ways of looking at progress: as a movement away from the start, or as a movement toward the goal. On the one hand, there is O-progress, defined in terms of increasing distance from the starting point (the "origin"). On the other hand, there is D-progress, defined in terms of decreasing distance from the goal (the "destination"). With any finitely distant goal these two are equivalent. But when the goal is infinitely removed, they are very, very different. Consider this picture:

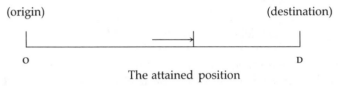

(origin)   (destination)

O   D

The attained position

Clearly, we here increase the distance traveled from O by exactly the same amount as we decrease the distance remaining to D. But if there is no attainable destination—if we are engaged on a journey that is, for all we know, literally endless and has no determinable destination, or only one that is "infinitely distant"— then we just cannot manage to decrease our distance from it. All we can ever do then is to make O-progress—to make still further improvements on our current position. The idea of approaching a goal becomes infinite. And it is just this sort of situation that is at issue with our human limitations. Struggling ahead to do what we can is the best that we can manage.

The Paradox of Finitude

How tragic for us is the fact of our finitude? Fortunately, things are not as bad as they might be. The saving paradox of the debility of finitude is that finitude provides its own remedy. The important—and ironic—fact is that it is our very limitedness that makes our limitations easier to bear.

If we were subject to no *temporal* limit, then—barring the miracle of perpetual regeneration—we would have to contemplate an unending gradual (asymptotic) decline after the bloom of youth. The limitation of time renders the limitation of our abilities easier to accept. If we had unlimited *resources*, then the limitation of talent and ability would clearly be even more painful. The ongoing struggle for our daily bread would not then provide a covering of sorts for our many other limitations. If we had no limitation of knowledge—if, for example, the time of our death were a known fact rather than a matter of uncertain speculation—then leading our lives in the normal happy-go-lucky way that we do would be very difficult indeed. Moreover, we are—mercifully—cognitively limited in such a way that we cannot say just what our limits are. In this way too ignorance is bliss. And so it goes. The very existence of our limitedness makes our limitations easier to bear.

Only if *all* of our limits and limitations were removed together, in their collective entirety, would the net result be a clear gain. And then of course we would transmute into something very different indeed and dwell among the gods of a (doubtless much improved) version of Mount Olympus. As it is, the removal of any single aspect of finitude by itself would be a source of endless grief.

It is a salient aspect of the human condition that we strive for the realization of our goals in the absence of any guarantee of success; we can virtually never know for sure in advance whether failure or success will attend our efforts. And because benefit by and large attaches to even merely making the effort—since often as not it is no less rewarding to try than to achieve—we are the better off for it. Our very limits make our limitations more bearable and help to alleviate the burdens of limitation. And even though taking this point of view may be "looking on the bright side of things," we had still better be glad for small mercies and welcome opportunities to make the best of a difficult situation.

NINE

The Quest of Sisyphus

THE IMPULSE to transcendence is an integral and formative aspect of the human condition. Faced with the reality of finitude, limitedness, and imperfection, we humans cannot be content to let matters rest there. We have the hubris to ask for more—ever to wish for, nay to *demand*, a definitiveness and finality at odds with the stark realities of our situation. In seeking to overcome the transiency and mortality that everywhere surrounds us, we become committed to an inexorably frustrated (and frustrating) unachievable quest—the search for something permanent and abiding in a world whose all-pervasive law is change.

The ancient Egyptians sought for permanence in physical form—in stone pyramids and mummified bodies. But the ravages of change were inexorable—the winds (or vandals) demolished the stonework; the robbers (or archaeologists) desecrated the graves.

The early Greeks, by contrast, sought permanence in immaterial structures—in mathematics (Pythagoras) and in the realm of abstract ideas (Plato). But this also proved problematic because these immaterial realms are too remote from reality. We cannot satisfactorily connect them with this world of ours—cannot provide any really intelligible account of mundane reality's "participation" in the eternal.

The Stoics proposed to see the world's transient phenomena as exemplifying permanent laws. They sought for a permanent realm of natural laws—an abiding structure of natural process within the very operation of the ever-changing multiplicity of nature's events. This project has proved more abiding. After the Middle Ages' venture into otherworldliness, the moderns since Galileo and Newton have adopted this Stoic program of seeking finality in the findings of science.

Yet the problem with such an approach has become all too clear over the years. The scientific search for "the laws of nature" is certainly a search for something permanent, something definitive and unchanging. But while those laws of nature as such—in and of themselves—may indeed possess such stability, all that *we* can ever obtain are our *beliefs* about those laws— our conjectures or suppositions about them. And these cognitive artifacts—these conjectures and suppositions of ours—are certainly nothing permanent. The substance structure of matter and the molecular structure of life may be permanent facts, but access to them is through the mediation of ever-changing conceptions. In the twentieth century, the rate of change in scientific theorizing at the frontier of discovery has become so strikingly swift as to defeat even the most determined efforts to ignore it. And in the wake of this, it has become painfully obvious that a sharp line must be maintained between the laws of nature *as such* (whatever these may be), and the *purported* laws of nature in whose terms we ourselves conduct our scientific business. Alas, whatever permanency the former may have is certainly not possessed by the latter.

The quest for transcendence that is typified by science's search for "the laws of nature" exemplifies a larger cognitive aspiration. Our search for cognitive access to something definitive, absolute, permanent—something that stands fixedly secure against the ravages of change, transiency, and destruction—takes many forms. The objectives at issue include, alongside the absolutely correct answer to the complex questions of scientific fact, such matters as

the definitive interpretation of complex literary texts or problematic historical episodes;
the perfect system of philosophical knowledge; and
the ultimately appropriate resolution of a perplexing issue of action.

Life sets a difficult task to the thinking person. And human nature equips us with a deep-rooted commitment to the idea of definitively correct answers to our theoretical and practical questions. By the very nature of human nature, inquiring minds come to be committed to the idea of finality. Each culture, each generation, each thinker is destined—or, perhaps, *condemned*—to the *search* for correct answers and definitive solutions. The idea of absoluteness projects a siren call that ever sways us in our problem-solving endeavors.

And yet we realize in our heart of hearts that this yearning is futile. We acknowledge that the scientists of the year 5,000 will think of the imperfections and inadequacies of our science much as we think of those of the science of Newton's day. We cannot but admit that the morally sensitive person of the year 3,000 will think that the treatment of proto-children, of old people, of the different and disadvantaged that we think of as perfectly acceptable are grossly deficient.

We are programmed to regard the best that we can do in investigation and reflection as being correct. And yet at some time we realize that what we accept as definitely correct is not really so. The inconsistency at issue, reflected in the so-called "Preface Paradox," is a paradigm of the human situation. The paradox has been formulated in the following terms:

Consider the writer who, in the Preface to his book, concedes the occurrence of errors among his statements. Suppose that in the course of his book a writer makes a great many assertions, which we shall call $s_1, \ldots, s_n$. Given each one of these, he believes that it is true. . . . However, to say that not everything I assert in this book is true, is to say that at least one statement in this book is false. That is to say that at least one of $s_1, \ldots, s_n$ is false; . . . that $(s_1 \& \ldots \& s_n)$ is false; that $\sim(s_1 \& \ldots \& s_n)$ is true. The author who writes and believes each of $s_1, \ldots s_n$ and yet in a preface asserts and believes $\sim(s_1 \& \ldots \& s_n)$ is, it appears, behaving very rationally. Yet clearly he is holding logically incompatible beliefs: he believes each of $s_1, \ldots, s_n, \sim(s_1 \& \ldots \& s_n)$, which form an inconsistent set. The man is being rational though inconsistent.[1]

[1] D. C. Makinson, "The Paradox of the Preface," *Analysis*, 25 (1964): 205–7. Compare H. E. Kyburg, Jr., "Conjunctivitis," in M. Swain, ed., *Induction, Acceptance, and Rational Belief* (Dordrecht, 1970), pp. 55–82, especially p. 77; and also R. M. Chisholm, *The Theory of Knowledge*, 2d ed. (Englewood Cliffs, N.J., 1976), pp. 96–97. The fundamental idea of the Preface Paradox goes back to C. S.

The fact is that in most of our problem-solving endeavors we are exactly in the position of the author of such a preface. We want to make all those statements—in the prevailing situation of the cognitive state of the art, we believe each and every one of them. But we also realize that sundry of them are false—we cannot, of course, say which—and that in the future many of them will have to be modified or rejected. Our overall stance is literally inconsistent.

Our interpretations of historical facts, our understanding of philosophical issues, our scientific explanation of nature's facts— indeed all of our cognitive endeavors—are all subject to ongoing and potentially unending change. We know full well that, no matter how thoroughly we do our cognitive work, the best-wrought question resolutions we can achieve today will become unstuck tomorrow—and then work will have to be done all over again. A labor of Sisyphus confronts us. No matter how energetically we push our work of question resolution up the mountain of hopefully settled knowledge, we face the fact that it will come tumbling down again.

Why not give up? Why not join the skeptics on their bench on the sidelines? Because our very nature will not let us. The ineluctable fate of our inner nature rules that we are *Homo sapiens*, *Homo quaerens*, a creature committed by its very nature to the quest for knowledge and understanding. There is that within our species that will not let us rest without doing the very best we can with the means at our disposal at securing a cognitive hold on the world about us. We stand committed—be it by way of dedication or by way of condemnation—to the effort to seek the holy grail of ultimate and definitive knowledge.

But the very passage of time—that remorselessly cruel force that sweeps away all of our best efforts at knowledge-gathering— also grants us release. For unlike Sisyphus himself, we have the blessing of finitude. The release of sleep gives us rest from the tasks of the day; the passage of one generation to another transmits the onus of the toilsome task to others.

Our commitment to the impossible task represented by the quest for definitive knowledge is ultimately neither comic

---

Peirce, who wrote: "that while holding certain propositions to be each individually perfectly certain, we may and ought think it likely that some of them, if not more, are false. *Collected Papers*, 5: 498.

(strictly Quixotic) nor genuinely tragic (strictly Sisyphean) in its nature. It is not absurd, but noble. For there is nothing inherently inappropriate in an unwillingness to settle for an imperfect reality—in matters of abstract theory and cognition, at any rate. What justifies our commitment to such a recognizably unattainable ideal is not a self-delusive belief in its actual realizability, but (somewhat paradoxically) its eminent utility. For it is through our commitment to this ideal that we gain the impetus (and courage) to dedicate ourselves to the ever-fruitful albeit never-completed task of striving to advance the frontiers of knowledge.

The irony of the situation is that the ancient Greeks were essentially right. Within the range of the world's realities, the things that are most nearly immortal are exactly the creations of our own minds—mathematics, poetry, ideas—the things that are not part of nature's furniture at all, but creatures of the realm of hypothesis and imagination. In the course of our disappointing cognitive endeavors to *find* in the "external world" something that transcends transiency, we have been able to devise within the "inner world" of thought various instrumentalities of artifice in whose terms we are able actually to *create* it. Ironically, it is the inventive rather than the apprehensive operations of the mind that provide our best access to the domain of things immortal.

TEN

Luck

EVEN AS "the best-laid plans of mice and men gang aft agley,"
so sometimes—no doubt more rarely—does the most haphazard effort yield a splendid success. Some people scheme, strive,
and struggle to achieve their ends—and fail to make even a
plausible start. Others have great benefits thrust into their hands
fortuitously. Fortune is fickle, smiling on some and scowling at
others without the least apparent rhyme or reason. Some are
lucky, and others unlucky. That is just how life goes.

The role of chance in human affairs was once the topic of ex-
tensive discussion and intensive debate among philosophers. In
Hellenistic Greece, theorists debated tirelessly about the role of
eimarmenē, the unfathomable fate that remorselessly ruled the affairs of men and gods alike, regardless of their wishes and actions.[1] The Church fathers struggled mightily to combat the
siren appeal of the idea of *fortuna*, and Saint Augustine detested
the very word fate.[2] The topic of good or bad fortune, along with
the related issue of the extent to which we can control our own
destinies in this world, was ardently controverted in classical antiquity and came to prominence again in the Renaissance. And

---

[1] Some earlier Greek speculations about the impetus of *tuchē* (chance) on
people's prospects for the good life are treated in Martha C. Nussbaum, *The Fra-
gility of Goodness* (Cambridge, Mass., 1986).

[2] He abhorred the word as being literally unintelligible. "Abhorremus praeci-
pue propter vocabulûm, quod non in se vera conservit intelligi." *De civitate dei*,
v. 9. For Augustine, all that occurs is part of God's plan. What we call "chance"
is simply a matter of human ignorance.

the topic undoubtedly has a long and lively future before it, since it is certain that, as long as human life continues, luck will play a prominent part in this domain.

Almost invariably, luck, good or bad, powerfully affects our lives. A chance encounter at a sporting event leads X into the career that constitutes her life's work. By whim, Y decides to eat at a certain restaurant and meets the woman who is to be the love of his life—or eats the food that will lay him low with stomach poisoning. An unanticipated traffic jam leads Z to miss a flight that crashes. Luck holds us all in an iron grip. There is no getting around the fact that much of what happens to us in life—much of what we do or fail to achieve or become—is a matter not of inexorable necessity or of deliberate contrivance, but one of luck, of accident or fortune. As Pascal trenchantly put it: "You find yourself in this world only through an infinity of accidents" (vous ne vous trouvez au monde que par une infinité de hazards), seeing that "your birth is due to a marriage, or rather to a series of marriages of those who have gone before you. But these marriages were often the result of a chance meeting, of words uttered at random, of a hundred unforeseen and unintended occurrences."[3] As Pascal saw it, our very lives are a gamble. And his famous Wager argument is in fact an invitation to think about the big issue of life in this world and the next in the manner of a gambler.

Luck unquestionably deals with different people very differently. But fortunately, there are many different sorts of human goods—riches, intelligence, good looks, an amiable disposition, artistic talent, and so on. Mercifully, a person dealt a short suit in one department may well get a long suit in another: one can be unlucky at the gaming table of worldly fame and still be lucky in love. In a way, money is the most democratic of goods. In contrast to good looks or intelligence or a healthy constitution, one does not have to be born into money, but can, with fortune's aid, acquire it as one goes along.

Luck marks the deep conflict between the actual and the ideal in this world. The most needy and deserving people do not, in general, win the lottery (and if they did, there would, ironically,

---

[3]"*Trois Discours sur la condition des grands*," in *Oeuvres complètes*, ed. Louis Lafuma (Paris, 1963), p. 366.

be no lotteries for them to enter). Luck is the shipwreck of utopias—the rogue force that prevents ideologues from leveling
the playing field of life. Only before God, the just law, and the
gravedigger is the condition of all alike and equal. Rationalistic-
minded philosophers have always felt uneasy about luck because it so clearly delimits the domain within which people have
control over their lives.

One way of reading the lesson urged by skeptics from classical antiquity to the present day is as follows: that no matter how
conscientiously we "play by the rules" in matters of factual inquiry, there is no categorical assurance that we will answer our
questions correctly. Even in science there is an ineliminable
prospect of a slip between evidence and generalization. Moreover, no less significantly—if more rarely—there can be epistemic windfalls: cases where we "play it fast and loose" as far
as the rules are concerned, and still get our answers right. Then
too there is the issue of "serendipity"—the finding of answers
to our questions or solutions to our problems by pure lucky
chance rather than by design, planning, contrivance, and the
use of sensible methods. In managing our information, as in
managing other issues in this life, luck can become a determinative factor.

Admitting that an element of unplannable unforeseeability
pervades all human affairs,[4] Renaissance humanists often inclined to the optimistic view that rational endeavor can prevail
against the slings and arrows of outrageous fortune. For example, Poggio Bracciolini (1380–1459), in his tracts *De miseria
humanae conditionis* and *De varietate fortunae*, championed the
efficacy of rational virtue: "The strength of fortune is never so
great that it will not be overcome by men who are steadfast and
resolute."[5] Fortune as such is no more than the product of the
interaction between human reason and nature's forces—both
products of God's endowment of his world. Others took a much
less sanguine line. Thus in Chapter 25 of *The Prince* (1513),

---

[4]"Nam rerum humanorum tanta est obscuritas varietasque, ut nihil dilucide
sciri possit." Erasmus, *Encom. Moral.*, xlv.

[5]For an illuminating discussion, see Antonino Poppi, "Fate, Fortune, Provi-
dence and Human Freedom," in C. B. Schmitt et al., eds. *The Cambridge History
of Renaissance Philosophy* (Cambridge, 1988), pp. 641–67. (The quotation is from
p. 653.)

Machiavelli, after surveying the cruelties and haphazards of the politics of his day, set more pessimistic limits to human endeavor by assigning half of what happens in this domain to the intractable power of Fortuna, though her rogue force might be partially tamed by prudently installed dikes and embankments.

What Is Luck?

What is luck? In characterizing a certain development as lucky for someone, we preeminently stake two claims:

1. That as far as the affected person is concerned, the outcome came about "by accident." (We would not claim that it was lucky for someone that his morning post was delivered to his house—unless, say, that virtually all of the mail was destroyed in some catastrophe, with some item of urgent importance for the person as one of a few chance survivors.)
2. That the outcome at issue has a significantly evaluative status in representing a good or bad result, a benefit or loss. (If X wins the lottery, that is good luck; if Z is struck by a falling meteorite, that is bad luck; but a chance event that is indifferent—say someone's being momentarily shaded by a passing cloud—is no matter of luck, one way or the other.)

Accordingly, the operation of luck hinges outcomes on what happens by accident rather than by design. Luck requires that the favorable outcome in view results not by planning or foresight but "by chance"—by causes impenetrable to us, or as the 1613 *Lexicon Philosophicum* of Goclenius put it, "depending not on the industry, insight, or sagacity of man, but on some other, altogether hidden cause" (non ab hominis industria et acumine iudicioque dependens, sed a causa alia occulta). Luck is a matter of our condition being affected, be it for good or ill, by developments that are neither intended nor foreseen, but lie substantially outside the domain of our control. But note that happy or unhappy developments can remain a matter of luck from the recipient's point of view even if its eventuation is the result of a deliberate contrivance by others. (Your secret benefactor's sending you that big check represents a stroke of good luck for *you* even if it is something that *he* has been planning for years.)

Luck fares rather mixedly in European languages. Greek *tuchē* is too much on the side of haphazard. In Latin, *fortuna* comes close to its meaning, with the right mixture of chance (*casus*) and benefit (be it positive or negative). But German has the misfortune that *Glück* means not only luck (*fortuna*) but also *happiness* (*felicitas*). The French *chance* (from the Latin *cadere* reflecting "how the dice fall") is a close equivalent of luck, however. And the Spanish *suerte* is also right on target. On the other side of the coin, several languages have a convenient one-word expression for specifically bad luck (French *malchance*, German *Pech*), a most useful resource, considering the nature of things, which English unaccountably lacks. (Despite its promising etymology, *misfortune* is not quite the same, since it embraces any sort of mishap, not merely those due to accident but also those due to one's own folly or to the malignity of others.)

Often—in lotteries, in marrying an heiress, or in escaping unscathed from an explosion thanks to the shielding of somebody else's body—one person's good luck can be attained at the cost of another's ill.[6] But good luck can also be victimless. If by some lucky stroke the world escapes an apocalyptic epidemic—or a nuclear war—everyone is lucky without any price paid by some unfortunates.

The core of the concept of luck is the idea of things going well or ill for us because of conditions and circumstances that lie wholly beyond our cognitive or manipulative control. Luck pivots on incapacity. In the affairs of an omniscient being who *knows* all outcomes, or of an omnipotent being that *controls* all outcomes, there is no scope for luck. (God is exempt from the operation of luck.)

A physical system is said to be chaotic when its processes are such that minute, effectively undetectable differences in an initial state can engender great differences in the result, with diminutive local variations amplifying into substantial differences in eventual outcomes. (The weather sometimes provides a fairly good example.) This sort of situation is pervasive in human affairs. Very small differences in how we act or react to what oc-

---

[6] As one German writer puts it, often "the guardian angels of those who have luck are the unlucky" (die Schutzengel derer, die Glück haben, sind die Verunglückten). Hans Pichler, *Persönlichkeit, Glück, Schicksal* (Stuttgart, 1967), p. 47.

curs about us can make an enormous difference in the result. A tiny muscle spasm can lead us to gasp and breathe in the germ that kills. The slightest change in timing can make the difference in buying a winning or a losing ticket in a lottery. Chaos (in this somewhat technical sense) pervades our human affairs and means that "luck"—that is, the impetus of *chance* on matters of human weal and woe—is destined to play a major role in our affairs.

Yet luck inheres even more prominently in cognitive than in physical limitations. Even in a causally (or, for that matter theologically) deterministic world, we can appropriately characterize as happening "by chance" *from our human point of view* those eventuations whose embedding in the world's causal (or rational) structure lies altogether beneath the threshold of any observations and discriminations that we could possibly manage to make. For then their rationalization (however real) could play no possible part in our deliberations and determinations. Accordingly—ontological determinism notwithstanding—such eventuations would figure in our thinking as matters of fortuitous chance. Their results are matters of "luck" *for us*, because (by hypothesis) no planning or foresight on our part can play even the slightest determinative role in the matter.

Can Luck Be Managed?

This aspect of incapacity is crucial. For one must avoid the tempting but catastrophic mistake of considering luck a harnessable force or agency in nature—or a power or talent of some sort that people can manage or manipulate.

The idea that luck is a somehow personified power or agency whose services can be enlisted and whose favor can be cultivated or lost is an ancient belief, reflected in classical antiquity by the conception of the goddess Fortuna (Greek Tuchē), often depicted on ancient coins as the bestower of prosperity, equipped with a cornucopia. Philosophers (especially Cicero) and theologians (especially the Church fathers) eloquently inveighed against this superstition—generally in vain. To be sure, the diffusion of Christian belief in an all-powerful deity countervailed against a mystical belief in luck. And post-Cartesian philosophy, with its increasing faith in scientific reason, reinforced this tendency among thinking people. Nonetheless, as with astrology and other ancient superstitions, the practice of seeking to win her favor by giving homage to "lady luck" has never been altogether extinguished.

The belief in an unlucky day (Friday the 13th),[7] a luck-producing object (a rabbit's foot), or a luck-controlling force (one's lucky star), turns on the idea that luck is something that can be promoted or influenced. But all this is mere superstition. It withdraws luck from the domain to which it belongs—that of uncontrollable chance or circumstance—and domesticates it to the more familiar and comfortable realm of the regular and manageable. But alas, if luck could be manipulated, then it would cease to be what it *ex hypothesi* is, namely *luck*. If luck could be managed, we would not have the proverb, "You can't beat a fool for luck."

Though (virtually by definition) we cannot control or manipulate the chance element in human affairs, we have certainly come to *understand* it better and thus to accommodate ourselves to it more effectively. The bachelor who moves from a job in a factory that employs only men into an office heavily staffed with unmarried women thereby obviously improves his chances of finding a wife and thus securing domestic bliss—or its opposite. The person who buys a lottery ticket at least creates the opportunity to win; one who does not has no chance. Luck is not a force or agency that we can manipulate by way of bribery or propitiation. But it is something we can control within limits, by modifying the way we expose ourselves to it.

There is certainly little, if any, point in "cursing one's luck" when ill fortune befalls us. There is no sensible alternative to acknowledging the futility and wastefulness of rage and resentment—as opposed to a constructive determination to work to shape a world where the likelihood of misfortunes and disasters is diminished. The workings of luck are beyond our reach; whether or not we will be lucky or unlucky is something over which—virtually by definition—we can have no control. But the scope or room for luck is something we can indeed influence. The student who works hard does not rely on luck to pass the examination. The traveler who maps the journey out in advance

---

[7] "El martes ni te cases ni te embarques" (Neither marry nor journey on the Tuesday), runs a Spanish proverb.

does not rely on luck to produce a helpful and knowledgeable person to show the way. Foresight, sensible precautions, preparation, and hard work can all reduce the extent to which we require luck for the attainment of our objectives. We can never eliminate the power of luck in our affairs—human life is unavoidably overshadowed by the threat of chaos. But we certainly can act so as to enlarge or diminish the extent of our reliance on luck in the pursuit of desired ends. There is everything to be said for striving to bend one's efforts into constructive lines and then—win, lose, or draw—taking rational satisfaction in this very fact of having done all one could. (Admittedly, there will be circumstances when this is pretty cold comfort—as when one finds oneself on a tumbril headed for the guillotine. But that is just life!)

What is regrettable about the superstitious management of luck—keeping track of one's unlucky days, carrying a rabbit's foot, thanking one's lucky stars, planning by odd numbers, and all the rest—is that it is counterproductive. It diverts time, energy, and effort away from the kind of effective planning and working that has some real chance of improving one's lot. For to some extent, a wise person is indeed in a position to manipulate luck—not via occult procedures but by thoughtful planning and sensible action.

In various contexts, the prudent person can pick and choose the risks that are incurred. There are, above all, three ways in which we can influence the element of luck in our lives:

1. *Risk avoidance.* People who do not court danger (who do not try to cross the busy roadway with closed eyes) need not count on luck to pull them through.

2. *Insurance.* People who take care to make proper provision against unforeseeable difficulties by way of insurance, hedging, or the like need not rely on luck alone as a safeguard against disaster.

3. *Probabilistic calculation.* People who try to keep the odds on their side—who manage their risks with reference to determinable probabilities—can thereby diminish the extent to which they become hostages to fortune.

Note, however, that in the main these represent means for guarding against bad luck and its consequences. The prospects we have for courting good luck are fewer, though there are indeed things we can do to put ourselves in its way. (Only by buying a ticket for the lottery can we possibly win it; by improving our qualifications we can increase the chances of securing a good job.) But the fact remains that, in this real world of ours, good luck can be managed only within the most narrow of limits.

To be sure, in one important regard a "superstitious" feeling that luck is "on one's side" in one's present endeavors can make a difference. This has no bearing—obviously—when one is involved in a position of pure chance (like playing the horses), but such a presentiment can certainly influence outcomes in circumstances where a feeling of confidence can affect performance. When a salesman is dealing with "a difficult customer" or a tennis player with a "tough opponent," the feeling that today is one's lucky day—that on this occasion success will come one's way even "against the odds"—can make a real difference for one's prospects. But, of course, this is less a matter of actual luck than of psychology.

We Americans are imbued with the can-do spirit. The attitude of fatalistic resignation is alien to us. We enthusiastically agree with the old Roman (Plautus) who said that sagacious people make their own luck or fortune ("Sapientis ipse fingit fortunam sibi"). And the fact that this is unquestionably an unrealistic *assertion* does not prevent it from being a sensible *attitude*. For when we toil in the way of our cognitive deficiencies, we generally cannot be certain what will happen if we really make the effort and try. And so, by making these confident efforts we increase the prospects of producing excellent though otherwise unexpectable results.

People can, accordingly, come to grips with luck in some promising ways. Perhaps most importantly, they can do this by taking sensible measures to shield themselves against the consequences of bad luck. Be it in lotteries or in business, in romance or in warfare, one can manage one's affairs so as to reduce reliance on luck alone to yield a favorable issue. For example, only the commander who maintains a strategic reserve is in a good position to take advantage of an unexpectedly created opportunity. Napoleon's well-known tendency to entrust commands to marshals whose records showed them to have "luck on their side" did not (in all probability) so much betoken superstition as a sensible inclination to favor those who had a demonstrated record for the sagacious management of risks in warfare. Chance favors the prepared—those who are so situated as to be in a position to seize opportunities created by chance.[8] Those on the lookout for unanticipated openings can best take full advantage of them when they occur.

Nevertheless it is necessary and important to bear in mind that one cannot rationally manage and manipulate particular, genuinely stochastic outcomes. For that would be a contradiction in terms: if they were responsive to causal manipulation, those eventuations would not really be matters of chance at all. The idea of the rational management of chance eventuations is an absurdity—which does not alter the circumstance that the rational management of the *opportunities* that chance may bring our way is a very real talent.

The issue of the extent to which society should make up for the vagaries of luck in their impact on the fortunes of its members is an interesting question of social philosophy.[9] One widely respected ethicist tells us that in the just social order, bad luck will be redressed in various regards, that "since inequalities of truth and natural endowment are undeserved, these inequalities are to be somehow compensated for."[10] Presumably this would be done by improving the lot of the unfortunates rather than by leveling everyone else down to their condition. If so, clearly, being born in the right place and time—in a society willing and able to afford this vast compensatory project—would itself be a massive stroke of luck. But should we even try somehow to compensate people for their unasked-for deficiencies in intelligence, talent, good looks, ambition, and "drive," or for their psychological hardships, medical disabilities, or difficult children? Even raising these questions brings a smile, because the list is in principle unending. Luck's complexity and scope in human exis-

[8] When the New York Mets won the 1969 World Series despite being generally viewed as the inferior team, some attributed this outcome to "mere luck." As reported by Arthur Daley in the *New York Times*, Branch Rickey rejected this imputation with the sage observation that "luck is the residue of design." James Tuite, ed., *Sports of the Times: The Arthur Daley Years* (New York, 1975), p. 285; I owe this reference to Tamara Horowitz.

[9] The question is interestingly discussed in Richard A. Epstein, "Luck," *Social Philosophy and Policy*, 6 (1988): 17–38.

[10] John Rawls, *A Theory of Justice* (Cambridge, Mass., 1971), p. 100.

tence are too large for manipulability. There is simply no way of leveling the playing field of life. Indeed, efforts in this direction are in good measure inherently self-defeating. In trying to compensate people for ill luck, we would surely create more scope for luck's operation. For whatever forms of compensation we adopted—money, increased privileges, special opportunities— are bound to be such that some people are in a better position to profit by them than others, so that luck expelled by the front door simply reenters by the back. Moreover, it is by no means clear that everyone would welcome such compensation. Many of us would look joylessly on the agents of the Commissariat of Equalization come to inform us of our awards for having an obnoxious personality or—to take a more philosophical example— for being egregiously devoid of common sense.

While social utopians would fain compensate for bad luck in this world, philosophers—characteristically less sanguine— have generally looked elsewhere for compensation: to the next world with the Church fathers, the unending long run with Leibniz, or the noumenal order with Kant. Throughout, recourse to a transcendental order betokens a sober recognition of the unavoidable role of luck in this world's scheme of things.

Bismarck said that God so arranged matters that fortune favors children, fools, and the United States of America. But of all the world's people, it is perhaps those of Spain who rely most heavily on luck. For gambling has long been a prominent facet of Spanish life. (The Lotéria Nacional, established by Carlos III in 1763, is the oldest of the existing national lotteries.) Official estimates indicate that the money spent on gambling in Spain currently amounts to some 15 percent of family income, making that country a world leader in this regard.[11] Spaniards widely view gambling not as a human weakness or vice, but as a plausible opportunity for improving their condition.

Can One Have Moral Luck?

It is a somewhat ironic fact of life that luck has a significant bearing not only upon the factual issue of what happens to us in

---

[11] *The Economist* (Aug. 29, 1987) p. 49. At the present writing, the largest-ever lottery is Spain's *el gordo* ("the fat one"), with a prize in excess of $100 million.

life, but also upon normative issues of moral appraisal.[12] And it does so at three levels.

Particular actions. Consider the case of the lucky villain who burgles the house of his grandfather, whom he knows to be absent on a long journey. Unbeknownst to him, however, the old gentleman has meanwhile died and made him his heir. The property he "steals" is thus his own—legalistically speaking, he has in fact done nothing improper, a benign fate has averted the wrong his actions might otherwise have committed. In his soul or mind—in his intentions—he is a wicked thief, but in actual fact he is quite guiltless of wrongdoing under the postulatedly accurate description of his act as one of "taking something that belongs to oneself."

By contrast, consider the plight of the hapless benefactor. To do a friend a favor, he undertook to keep her car for her during an absence on a long journey. At around the expected time, the car is reclaimed by the friend's scheming identical twin—of whose existence our good-natured helper had no inkling. With all the goodwill in the world he has—by a bizarre act of unhappy fate—committed the misdeed of giving one person's entrusted property over to another. In intention he is as pure as the driven snow, but in actual fact he has fallen into wrongdoing.

Such cases illustrate how particular actions of a certain moral orientation can misfire because of the intervention of fortuitous circumstances. It is, in fact, considerations of exactly this sort that lead Kant to put such moral accidents on the agenda of ethical theorizing. For him, they furnish decisive indications that consequentialism will not do—that we must assess the moral status of actions on the basis not of their actual *consequences* but largely on the basis of their *intentions*. As Kant sees it, *moral* status and stature are wholly determined by what one wittingly tries to do and not by one's success, by actual performance. And there is much to be said for this view. But things can also be said against it. This becomes clear when we turn to the next item.

Courses of action. Consider the case of the night watchman of a bank who abandons his post of duty in order to go to the aid of a

[12] Compare Thomas Nagel, "Moral Luck," in his *Mortal Questions* (Cambridge, Mass., 1979), pp. 24–38; and also Bernard Williams's essay on the topic in his collection *Moral Luck* (Cambridge, Mass., 1982), pp. 20–39.

child being savagely attacked by a couple of men. If the incident is "for real," we see the night watchman as a hero. However, if the incident is a diversion stage-managed as part of a robbery, we see the night watchman as an irresponsible dupe. And yet from *his* point of view there is no visible difference between the two cases. How the situation turns out for him is simply a matter of luck.

In this way, various courses of action acquire an appraisal status that depends largely or wholly on how matters turn out—whether this is something that lies largely or wholly outside the agent's sphere of control. Human life is paved with such pitfalls. This seems to underscore the Kantian position.

But does it actually do so? To clarify the matter further, let us now shift attention from action to character.

Moral qualities. Character traits—moral ones included—are dispositional in nature, relating to how people *would* act in certain circumstances. For example, candor and generosity represent morally positive dispositions, dishonesty and distrust negative ones.

But note that a person can be saved from the actual consequences of malign dispositions by lack of opportunity. In a society of adults—in a mining camp, say, or on an oil rig—the child molester has no opportunity to ply his vice. Again, the very model of dishonesty can cheat no one when, Robinson Crusoe–like, he lives shipwrecked on an uninhabited island—at any rate until the arrival of man Friday.

Perhaps all of us are to some extent in this sort of position—are moral villains spared through lack of opportunity alone from discovering our breaking point, learning our price. As Schopenhauer somewhere observed, the Lord's Prayer's petition, "Lead us not into temptation," could be regarded as a plea for matters so to arrange themselves that we need never discover the sorts of people we really are.

To be sure, we generally hold people morally responsible only for what they actually *do.* But from the moral point of view, how people think and how they are disposed count every bit as much. The person who is prevented by lack of opportunity alone from displaying jealousy, envy, or greed still remains at heart a jealous (envious, greedy) person and (by hypothesis) merits the condemnation of those right-thinking people who know this to be so (say, on the basis of talk rather than action). Morality encompasses more than action.

This helps to explain why it is that while the coward can excuse himself by pleading his nature, his naturally timorous disposition, the immoralist cannot comparably plead *his* natural disposition and expect his innate cupidity, avarice, lecherousness, or the like to get him off the moral hook. For in such a case it is exactly his disposition that condemns him. (The fact that he did not come by his disposition by choice is immaterial; dispositions just are not the sort of thing that comes up for selective choice.)[13]

Of course, the point cuts both ways. The virtuous person can be preempted from any manifestation of virtue by uncooperative circumstance. Here is the moral hero primed for benign self-sacrifice—prepared at any moment to leap into the raging flood to save the drowning child. But fate has cast him into an arid and remote oasis, as devoid of drowning children as Don Quixote's Spain was lacking in damsels in distress. To be sure, we would be unlikely to *recognize* this heroism in either sense of the term. On the one hand, we would be unlikely to *learn* of it. And on the other, we would—even if evidence came our way—be ill-advised to *reward* it in the absence of circumstances that brought it into actual operation. (For one thing, we would not be confident that it is actually strong enough not to break under the pressure of an actual need for its manifestation.)

In any event, the fact remains that the role of luck in moral matters has the consequences that the lives we actually lead—including all the actions we actually perform—need not in fact reflect the sorts of persons we really are. In the moral domain, as elsewhere, luck can obtrude in such a way that—be it for good or for bad—people simply do not get the sort of fate they deserve. And this specifically includes our moral fate too—for good or ill, we may never be afforded the opportunity of revealing our true moral colors to the world at large.

---

[13] But is not one's disposition a matter of uncontrollable luck? Perhaps. But that, of course, does not affect the matter. If one comes by one's boldness by ill luck, one is still bold. And this holds for morality too. We hold people responsible for their moral character, not because we believe that they somehow make it for themselves, but because this is part of the fundamental moral presumption involved in treating a person as a person.

What does this mean? Does it mean (as Kant thought) that morality is not of this world—that moral appraisal requires making reference to an inaccessible noumenal order that stands wholly outside this empirical sphere of ours? Surely not!

We must form our moral judgments not on the basis of what happens *transcendentally* in an inaccessible noumenal order, but rather on the basis of that most prosaic of all suppositions— namely, that things happen as they *generally and ordinarily* do, that matters take the sort of course that it is only plausible to expect.

Moral evaluation as we actually practice it generally reflects the *ordinary* course of things. *Ordinarily*, breaking and entering is a wicked thing to do. *Ordinarily*, leaving one's post to help someone in need is a good thing. *Ordinarily*, driving drunk increases the chance of harm to others. *Ordinarily*, mendacious people cause pain when they scatter lies about them. *Ordinarily*, people ultimately get to manifest their true colors. Moral appraisals are *standardized* in being geared to the situation of the ordinary, common run of things. Admittedly luck, be it good or bad, can intrude in such a way as to prevent matters from running in the tracks of ordinariness. And then things go wrong. Moral acts that normally lead to the good can issue in misfortune. But that is just "tough luck." It does not—or should not— affect the issue of moral appraisal.

People who drive their cars home from an office party in a thoroughly intoxicated condition, indifferent to the danger to themselves and heedless of the risks they are creating for others, are equally guilty in the eyes of *morality* (as opposed to *legality*) whether they kill someone along the way or not. Their transgression lies in the very fact of their playing Russian roulette with the lives of others. Whether they actually kill someone or not is simply a matter of luck—of accident and sheer statistical haphazard. But the moral negativity is much the same one way or the other—even as the moral positivity is much the same one way or the other for the person who bravely plunges into the water in an attempt to save a drowning child. Regardless of outcome, the fact remains that, in the ordinary course of things, careless driving puts people's lives at risk unnecessarily, and rescue attempts improve their chances of survival. What matters for morality is the ordinary tendency of actions rather than their actual results under unforeseeable circumstances in particular cases.

One recent writer flatly denies this (after all, some philosophers will deny anything!). He writes:

> Whether we succeed or fail in what we try to do [in well-intentioned action] always depends to some extent on factors beyond our control. This is true of . . . almost any morally important act. What [is accomplished] and what is morally judged is partly determined by external factors. However jewel-like the good will may be in its own right, there is a morally significant difference between actually rescuing someone from a burning building and dropping him from a twelfth story window while trying to rescue him.[14]

The difference our author speaks of is indeed there. But only because of a lack of specificity in describing the case. Preeminently, we need to know *why* it was that our rescuer dropped the victim. Was it from carelessness or incompetence or a sudden flash of malice? Or was it because, despite all due care on his part, Kant's "unfortunate fate" intervened and a burnt-out timber gave way under his feet?[15] If so, then Kant's assessment surely prevails. Where a moral agent's success or failure is differentiated only and solely by matters of pure luck, then there is patently no reason for making different *moral* appraisals one way or the other.[16]

[14] Nagel, "Moral Luck," p. 25.

[15] "Even if it should happen that, by a particularly unfortunate fate or by the niggardly provision of a stepmotherly nature, this [good] will should be wholly lacking in power to accomplish its purpose, and if even the greatest effort should not avail it to achieve anything of its end, and if there remained only the good will (not as a mere wish but as the summoning of all the means in our power), it would sparkle like a jewel in its own right, as something that had its full worth in itself." Immanuel Kant, *Foundations of the Metaphysics of Morals*, sec. 1, para. 3.

[16] To say this is not of course to say that we may not want to differentiate such situations on *non-moral* grounds—e.g., to reward only *successful* rescues or to punish only *realized* transgressions as a matter of social policy *pour encourager les autres*. Compare also Bernard Williams's example of the person who abandons a life of service to others in order to pursue his art—a decision whose moral justification (according to Williams) will ultimately hinge on how good an artist he turns out to be, which largely depends not on effort, but on talent and creative vision, issues at the mercy of nature's allocation over which he has no control (*Moral Luck*, pp. 24ff). But what earthly reason is there for seeing the *moral* situation of the talented Gauguin as being in this regard different from that of the incompetent Ignaz Birnenkopf? The impropriety of an abandonment of a moral obligation is not negated by the successes it facilitates on other fronts. Kant's point that the talented and untalented, the lucky and the unlucky, should

This Kantian idea goes straight back to the Greek tradition. Greek moralists were generally attracted to the following line. How *happy* we are will in general be a matter of accident. *Hēdonē* is chancy business; pleasure is bound to depend on chance and fortune—on the fortuitous opportunities that luck places at our disposal. If fate treats one adversely enough, then one may simply be unable to realize the condition of affective happiness (as counterdistinguished from rational satisfaction). Chance plays a predominant role here—circumstances beyond one's control can be decisive. But our virtue is something that lies within our own control and thus reflects our real nature. And this holds quite in general for the achievement of well-being along the lines of the Greek *eudaimonia*.[17] One is entitled to take rational satisfaction in a life lived under the guidance of sound values irrespective of how circumstances eventuate in point of happiness. One's affective *happiness* lies in the hands of the gods, but one's moral *goodness* is something that lies in one's own power.

Here Kant is surely right in following the lead of the Greeks. Morality as such is impervious to luck: no matter how things eventuate, the goodness of the good act and the good person stands secure from the vagaries of outcomes. But Kant's *analysis* of this situation went wrong. If morality prescinds from luck, this is not because morality contemplates the *ideal* situation of a *noumenal* sphere, but because morality contemplates the *normal* situation of the *ordinary course of things* in this mundane sphere of our quotidian experience, a course from which the *actual* sequence of events can and often does depart.

There is, to be sure, some good reason for viewing the failed and the successful rescue in a different light. For—by hypothesis—we know of the person who brings it off successfully that he has actually persevered to the end, whereas the person whose efforts were aborted by a mishap might possibly have abandoned them before completion for discreditable motives such as fecklessness, folly, or fear. We recognize, after all, that an ele-

---

stand equal before the tribunal of morality is well taken, and Hegel's idea that great men stand above and outside the standards of morality has little plausibility from "the moral point of view."

[17] This concept, which is prominent in Aristotle, goes back to Democritus. See J. C. B. Gosling and C. C. W. Taylor, *The Greeks on Pleasure* (Oxford, 1982), pp. 29–30.

ment of uncertainty pervades all human activities, and an uncharacteristic flash of inconstancy might possibly deflect someone in the process of performing a worthy act. But if we did somehow know for certain—as in real life we never do—that, but for circumstances beyond his control, the agent would indeed have accomplished the rescue, then we will have no basis for denying moral credit. Our reluctance to award full credit has its grounding in considerations that are merely epistemic and not moral. I submit that in *this* regard Kant's perception was quite right.

Thus consider a somewhat variant case—that of the brave woman who leaps into the raging waters (or the flaming inferno) to save a trapped child. Only after the fact does she learn that it was her own. Had she known it all the time, she would indeed have got full marks for motherly solicitude—since in the circumstances we would have to presume that it was this, rather than disinterested humanitarianism, that provided the motive. But once we establish that she had no way of realizing this at the time, we have to award her full moral credit.

To be sure, with a little novelistic imagination we can all envision bizarre circumstances in which the exercise of the standard virtues (truth-telling, kindness, etc.) repeatedly produces disastrous effects. But their status as virtues is geared to the standard course of things—how matters *standardly* and *ordinarily* go in their actual world. It is because morality is geared to the world's ordinary course of things that heroic action is not a demand of morality but a matter of supererogation. (And it is this, of course, that is the Achilles heel of Kant's analysis.)

It is in fact not difficult to construct examples that illustrate the advantages of the present normalcy-averted approach as compared with Kant's noumenal perspective. Consider the case of Simon Simple, a well-intentioned but extremely foolish lad. Thinking to cure Grandmother's painful arthritis, Simon bakes her for twenty minutes at 400 degrees Fahrenheit in the large family oven. He labors under the idiotic impression that prolonged exposure to high temperatures is not only not harmful to people but actually helpful in various ways—curing arthritis among them. His *intentions* are nothing other than good. Yet few sensible moralists would give Simon a gold star. For he should know what any ordinary person knows: that broiling people medium well by prolonged exposure to temperatures of 400 degrees is bad for them. We base our moral judgment on the ground rules of the ordinary case, and Simon's good intentions simply do not get him off the hook here. (That is just another aspect of his bad luck.)

What has been said here about the relationship of luck to morality holds for the relationship between luck and practical rationality as well. Even if performing a certain action is in fact conducive to realizing your appropriate ends (if, say, ingesting yonder chemical substance will actually cure your illness), it is nevertheless *not* rational so to act if you have no knowledge of this circumstance (and all the less so if such information as you have points the other way). Even when we happen by luck or chance to do what is, in the circumstances, the best thing to do, we have *not* acted rationally if we have proceeded without having any good reason to think that our actions would prove appropriate—let alone if we had good reason to think that they would be inappropriate. The agent who has no good reason to think that what she does conduces to her appropriate ends is not acting rationally. And this deficiency is not redeemed by unmerited good fortune—by luck's having it that things turn out all right. Rationality in action is not a matter of acting *successfully* toward our ends, but one of acting *intelligently*, and, given the role of chance in the world's events, these are not necessarily the same.

In sum, while the role of luck may be decisive for the *consequences* of our actions, it is not so for their evaluative status, be it rational or moral.

Do People Deserve Luck?

Can someone have deserved or undeserved good luck? Of course. Good luck often comes to the unworthy, ill luck to those who deserve better. But if genuine *luck* is at issue (with its admixture of real fortuitous chance), then it would always be a mere superstition to contemplate the matter in retributively causal terms—to think that people come by their good or bad luck because they somehow deserve it. In normal circumstances, what ultimately matters for the moral enterprise is not achievement but endeavor. And it is exactly this that prevents luck from being a crucial factor here. Luck, be it good or ill, generally comes to people uninvited and unmerited. Life is unfair—and luck is, above all, the reason why. The key lesson here is once again Kant's. We would do well to see luck and fortune as extraneous factors that do not bear on the moral assessment of a person's character. What actually happens to us in life is generally in substantial measure a product of luck and fate—of "circumstances beyond our control."

It is crucially important, then, to recognize the role of luck in human affairs—for good and ill alike. For otherwise one succumbs to the gross fallacy of assimilating people's characters to their actual lots in life. It is the recognition of luck, more than any other single thing, that leads us to appreciate the contingency of human triumphs and disasters. "There but for some stroke of luck go I" is a humbling thought whose contemplation is salutary for us all. One cannot properly appreciate the human realities so long as one labors under the adolescent delusion that people get the fates they deserve. During every century of the existence of our species, this planet has borne witness to a measureless vastness of unmerited human suffering and cruelly unjust maltreatment of people by one another. Only in exceptional circumstances is there any linkage between the normative issue of the sorts of people we are and the factual issue of how we fare in this world's course of things. The disconnection of the two factors of fate and desert, which luck so clearly signalizes, is a fact of life—a perhaps tragic but nevertheless characteristic and inescapable feature of the human condition.[18]

[18] This chapter constituted the author's Presidential Address to the American Philosophical Association (Eastern Division) in December 1989.

Two Modes of Morality

A PLAUSIBLE case can be made for contending that present-day Anglo-American moral theorists are doing only part of their job. By focusing their attention almost entirely on actions that safeguard the interests of others, they are neglecting half of the overall task that has historically constituted the defining mandate of their discipline. The nature and the implications of this situation deserve closer attention.

Beginning with Plato, the moralists and moral theorists of Greek antiquity occupied themselves with two ultimately not so very different objects of concern: the self and others. The cardinal aim of ethics, as Aristotle insisted, is to aid us to become good people,[1] and this involves goodness both in relation to others and in relation to ourselves. From the very outset, accordingly, there have been two dimensions of morality, one geared to *benevolence*, and the other to *self-development or self-realization*.

Benevolence morality (B-morality) deals with those aspects of the conduct of rational agents that relate to their doing right or wrong in their interactions with other people. Its forefront problem is, "Do the individual's decisions about actions take proper account of the interests of others?" Throughout its province, the issue of other-concerning conduct is primary. Benevolence ethics deals with such other-directed social virtues as honesty, reliability, probity, truthfulness, justice, civility, tolerance, and

---

[1] *Nicomachean Ethics*, II, 2.

forebearance. This domain is concerned throughout with our obligations to others.

By contrast, self-development or self-realization morality (S-morality) has to do with an individual's conduct in self-concerning matters. Its focus is on the axiological question, "What endows life with worth and value?" The considerations at issue here are posed by such questions as these: what sort of life should we be trying to create for ourselves? What kind of lifestyle would we, as sensible people, ideally want for ourselves—or, perhaps, to focus the issue less egocentrically, for our children? What manner of existence should we be pleased and proud to find a long-lost offspring leading? Throughout this sphere, the forefront problem is, "Do the individual's decisions about action take proper account of his or her own genuinely best (or real or true) interests?" The province of this mode of morality is self-realization and its concern is with *eudaimonia*, a person's human well-being or flourishing. The object here is to achieve a life that is "successful" not in terms of money or power, but in more broadly *axiological* terms—that is, in the realization in and for oneself of the appropriate values that are attainable given one's place in the world's scheme of things. The crux is value-realization, the achievement of those things that are for a person's best or real interests. Self-realization ethics, accordingly, encompasses such self-directed personal virtues as cultivation, diligence, ambition, consistency, dignity, and self-respect. Its prime concern is with the good life—the sort of life in which one justifiably takes rational satisfaction.[2]

Such a perspective is a reminder that benevolence morality, however important, is not enough. One can meet all its demands in one's relations with others and still lead a life that is impoverished and barren in matters of self-realization and self-development. The life of a person who behaves morally toward others is one thing; a good and truly rewarding and worthwhile life is something else again, something that—perhaps unfortunately—is not necessarily encompassed in a benevolently moral life.

From the very outset of the discipline, ethics has been a domain that embraces both sides of this dichotomy: both the other-

---

[2]Think of Aristotle's thesis that "estin hē eudaimonia psuchēs energeia tis kat'aretēn teleian." Ibid., I, 13, 1102b5.

regarding *social* virtues and the *personal* virtues of self-realization and self-development. Both of these moral concerns represent fundamentally normative enterprises, whose business is not with what people happen to want, but with what it would make good rational sense for them to want, given their nature and their situation. And both deal with parts of a single whole: the principles for the appropriate conduct of one's life in relation to people in general, oneself included.

It deserves emphasis that the issues of self-realization morality, like those of benevolence morality, are normative rather than descriptive. Their identification does not proceed by way of an *empirical* investigation into the doings of particular people who are generally deemed to be virtuous. Rather, they are to be identified through their concern with the *evaluative* issue of the sorts of conditions and circumstances under which people are rationally entitled to take satisfaction in the conditions of their lives and the character of their actions. Self-realization morality focuses on proper care for what one makes of oneself through one's own actions. The crux is the normative matter of one's rational entitlement to be content with one's doings.

The precepts of self-realization morality, like those of benevolence morality, are essentially universal in that they hold for rational agents in general. As deontologists since Kant's day have emphasized, such other-oriented moral desiderata as keeping one's promises, fulfilling one's obligations, and avoiding deceit are morally appropriate in a strictly universal way, not just for humans but for *any* rational agent. And exactly such universality also holds good for the desiderata of self-oriented morality. It is appropriate not just for humans, but for any rational agent to

> make good use of its intelligence;
> develop (some of) its talents and abilities for positive achievement;
> endeavor to realize its potential for the good;
> interact with (some) others in ties of friendship, familial affection, or love;
> make some constructive contribution to the world's work.

As Kant puts it, in discussing "the duties of man to himself" in part 2 of *The Metaphysics of Morals*: "It is a duty of man to himself to cultivate his natural powers. . . . Man owes it to himself (as an intelligent being) not to leave unused his talents and capacities (of what his reason may someday need to make use), leaving them, as it were, to rust."[3] "Do the right things by yourself" is no less appropriately imperative a commandment than "Do the right things by others." What *The Encyclopaedia* of Diderot and d'Alembert says of justice in particular holds for morality in general: it is "a virtue that makes us render to God, to ourselves, and to other men what is each their due" (un vertu qui nous fait rendre à Dieu, à nous-mêmes, et aux autres hommes ce qui leur est du à chacun). To fail willfully and systematically in one's benevolence-oriented duties to others makes one into a wicked person who is effectively *inhuman*. But to fail willfully and systematically in one's self-oriented duties makes one *subhuman*. Both sorts of failure—self-neglect along with negligence toward the claims of others—are not just regrettable but *wrong*. Someone who willfully and frivolously neglects to care for his or her own best interests is not just imprudent but wicked. One would remonstrate with such a person much as one would remonstrate with someone who inflicts injury on another. And in some cases—paternalistic ones, to be sure—one would even think that punishment is deserved.[4]

Some may, of course, object: "How can one possibly endorse this idea of *moral duties* to oneself? Surely whatever sort of '*commitment*' is at issue in such cases is not really a *duty*." In responding, two observations are in order. Why should one *not* speak of a "duty" here? Where is it written that "duties" have to be other-directed and that there cannot be self-oriented obligations? But to those who would still unyieldingly insist that duties must, as such, involve the interests of others, the response is this: feel free to reinterpret these "duties to oneself" as highly diffused "duties one owes to one's environing human community or to people at large." That self-neglect deprives others

<hr>

[3] *Akad.*, 6: 444.

[4] However, once one sees people who do not care for their own well-being as no longer teachable, one would be reluctant to impose sanctions on them out of a sensible reluctance to make a bad situation worse. (The reformist rationale of punishment for wrong inflicted on others has a plausible counterpart for self-inflicted wrongs, but deterrence will carry over only in small part, and retribution not at all.)

(relatives, fellow citizens, interested bystanders, people at large) of the better version of oneself that ought to be at their disposal. But these are perhaps technicalities. Let us return to basics.

Moral philosophy as a whole is a complex venture in which both questions, how we do by others (our other-oriented virtues) and how we do by ourselves (our self-oriented virtues), are matters of appropriate concern. Both benevolence ethics and self-realization ethics form integral parts of morality's overall mandate. And indeed, even single-track benevolence moralists cannot really avoid coming to grips with the matter of personal development at issue in self-realization, since their care for the benefit of people is bound to project into this area of what actually is best for people. The question of "the good of a person" is a crucial matter for a morality of any sort.

The Greek Heritage

The ancient Greeks saw all this quite clearly. As Table 7 indicates, there are three very different (albeit doubtless interrelated) issues, geared to goodness, pleasure, and wisdom, that the Greek moralists contemplated as the status of the *virtuous*, the *happy*, and the *wise* man, respectively. The second of these issues, pleasure—the concern of prudence—is generally placed outside the domain of morality proper, which consists of the first and last alone. In the field of moral theory, then, our bequest from the Greeks is a view that featured three sorts of goods: (moral) virtue or moral goodness (*aretē*); affective happiness or pleasure (*hēdonē*); and rational contentment or reflective happiness (*eudaimonia*).

Now the Greeks saw moral virtue and reflective happiness as closely interconnected. As they viewed the matter, it is only by being generally virtuous that we rational beings can properly achieve reflective contentment with ourselves. And truly virtuous persons are well rounded: they must both honor what is due to others and do what is right and fitting *for themselves*.[5] Accordingly, virtue and reflective happiness were taken as more or less different sides of the same coin. As for pleasure (*hēdonē*),

[5] For a good treatment of all these issues in Greek moral thought, see J. C. B. Gosling and C. C. W. Taylor, *The Greeks on Pleasure* (Oxford, 1982).

TABLE 7

Issues of Moral Concern

Type of good	Key question involved
Moral virtue, goodness, *aretē*, *virtus*	*Sittlichkeit*: Does the person in question lead a (morally) *good* life?
Affective happiness, pleasure, euphoria, *hēdonē*, *voluptas*	*Glücklichkeit*: Does the person in question lead a *happy* or *enjoyable* life?
Rational contentment, reflective happiness, *eudaimonia*, *beautitudo*	*Glückseligkeit*: Does the person in question lead a genuinely *satisfying and rewarding* life?

the odd man out, the Epicureans alone wanted to attribute moral significance to it. But as Cicero observed in *De finibus*, they had the unfortunate tendency to talk up a hard-line hedonism in *expounding* their views, only to fall back on a softer, eudaimonistic-sounding line when *defending* it—usually via a quick retreat from carnal to intellectual pleasures.

In general, the moral theoreticians of Greek antiquity were inclined to give self-realization morality precedence over benevolence morality. They were more concerned about the sorts of things people should be doing in order to lead worthwhile and satisfying lives than about the issue of what people owed to one another. "Happy is he" (*fortunatus ille*) was a thought that in one way or another was always in their minds. The task of moral philosophy, as seen by the Greeks, was primarily the articulation of a "philosophy of life"—a set of principles for conducting a truly satisfying life. The achievement of *eudaimonia* as a whole—of rational self-satisfaction—was seen as crucial, and the cultivation of specifically other-oriented moral virtue was often pictured as a merely subsidiary component or constituent of this. Only what was virtuous could be genuinely beneficial—mere pleasure as such was a hollow good.

This view of the matter came to form part of the mainstream of Western moral thought. And not only among Stoics and Christians. Take Spinoza, for example. No reader of his *Ethics* can fail to remark that for Spinoza the entire matter of our treatment of others in morally appropriate ways is just a side effect or incidental benefit of our achieving for ourselves the advantages of a life lived by acting "by the guidance of reason" (*ex ductu ra-tionis*). As he sees it, we are to act morally not simply because this is dutiful but ultimately because it is a demand of our rational nature. Moral comportment toward others is just another instance falling under the principle that "things are good only insofar as they aid man to enjoy that life of the mind that is determined by intelligence" (res eatenus tantum bonae sunt, quatenus homimem iuvant, ut Mentis via fruatur, quae intelligentia definitur).[6] Spinoza is thus at one with the mainstream of Greek moral thought in treating benevolence morality as a mere appendage of self-realization morality. Like the majority of Greek moralists, he believed that a virtuous man was entitled to rational contentment regardless of how fate and fortune treated him, seeing that "blessedness is not the reward of virtue, but virtue itself" (Beatitudo non est virtutis praemium, sed ipsa virtus).[7]

Kant

Perhaps the most effective and efficient way of protecting the best interests of people in general is to get everyone to exercise an appropriate concern for his own best interests. Traditionally then, Western moral theorists have been concerned with *both* benevolence *and* self-realization, with pride of place being accorded to the latter. And this approach prevailed as late as Kant, who, seeing morality as a matter of duty, was deeply concerned both with one's duties to others and with one's duties toward oneself.

It is worthwhile to quote at some length from Kant's rather discursive *Lectures on Ethics*.[8] Kant sets out his position in the following terms in the section on "Duties to Oneself":

He who transgresses against himself loses his humanity and becomes incapable of doing his duty towards his fellows. A man who performed his duty to others badly, who lacked generosity, kindness and sympa-

[6] *Ethics*, book 4, Appendix, chap. 5.
[7] Ibid., book 4, prop. 42.
[8] The *Vorlesungen über Ethik* were not published until long after his death, as part of the Berlin Academy edition (1924). For an English rendition, see *Immanuel Kant: Lectures on Ethics*, tr. Louis Infeld (Indianapolis, 1980).

thy, but who nevertheless did his duty to himself by leading a proper life, might yet possess a certain inner worth; but he who has transgressed his duty towards himself can have no inner worth whatever. . . . It follows that the precondition of our duty to others is our duty to ourselves; we can fulfill the former only insofar as we first fulfill the latter. Let us illustrate our meaning by a few examples of failure in one's duty to oneself. A drunkard does no harm to himself, yet he is an object of contempt. . . . A boastful liar, even though by his lies he does no harm to anyone, yet becomes an object of contempt; he throws away his personhood; his behavior is vile, he has transgressed his duty towards himself. . . . We must also be worthy of our humanity; whatsoever makes us unworthy of it makes us unfit for anything, and we cease to be men. . . .

Our duties towards ourselves constitute the supreme condition and the principle of all morality; for moral worth is the worth of the person as such; our capacities have a value only in regard to the circumstances in which we find ourselves. Socrates lived in a state of wretchedness; his circumstances were worthless; but though his circumstances were so ill-conditioned, yet he himself was of the highest value. Even though we sacrifice all life's amenities we can make up for their loss and sustain approval by maintaining the worth of our humanity. We may have lost everything else, and yet still retain our inherent worth. Only if our worth as human beings is intact can we perform our other duties; for it is the foundation stone of all other duties. A man who has destroyed and cast away his personhood, has no intrinsic worth, and can no longer perform any manner of duty. . . .

All such duties are grounded in a certain love of honor consisting in self-esteem; man must not appear unworthy in his own eyes; his actions must be in keeping with humanity itself if he is to appear in his own eyes worthy of inner respect. To value approbation is the essential ingredient of our duties towards ourselves.[9]

For Kant, then, as this passage makes transparently clear, our duty of self-realization is absolutely fundamental for ethics in general, seeing that respect for personhood in ourselves is the indispensable precondition and foundation for the respect of personhood in others. However, this individualistic-sounding starting point did not impede Kant's ethics from making a transit to the level of generality via his Categorical Imperative. And with Kant's successors, this dedication to generality became decisive. However, their concern for the level of generality often led to a downplaying of the significance of the individual person. The utilitarians must take credit (or blame) for this.

[9] *Immanuel Kant: Lectures on Ethics*, pp. 118–25.

Utilitarianism

Jeremy Bentham was born in 1748, within a year of Kant's first publication in 1747. It was not so long after the rise of the Kantian deontological philosophy, then, that utilitarianism came along, with its supreme moral principle of "the greatest good of the greatest number." This populist standard led the utilitarians straightaway to a virtual dismissal of the individual self as a separate item of significant moral concern. For we ourselves are—clearly—a mere drop in the vast sea of humanity at large. A morality of the greatest good of the greatest number swiftly pushes the self off the pedestal of special consideration.

The great impact that utilitarianism exerted in the Anglo-Saxon world—even on people who were not themselves utilitarians—led to the virtual disappearance of self-realization ethics in this sphere. Ethics took a social and statistical turn. The old aristocratic-sounding standard of self-development came to be replaced by a more democratic dedication to public-spiritedness and the promotion of the general good.

This phenomenon is strikingly clear in our own place and time. One illustration among many others is afforded by recent text anthologies for undergraduate college courses in "applied ethics." They invariably offer selections relating to the morality of taking life (suicide, euthanasia, abortion, capital punishment, war) and the morality of creating life (sexual ethics, contraception, obligations to future generations). They often also consider various issues of morality in our dealings with others (business ethics, professional ethics, familial obligations, etc.). And of course issues of social justice loom large (racism, affirmative action, distributive justice, censorship). Sometimes, too, our supposed moral obligations outside the human domain come in (animal rights, environmental ethics, etc.). But we ourselves as self-responsible agents are seldom on the agenda.[10] Only rarely is there material dealing with matters of self-realization—with the duty for people, say, to develop their talents, broaden their interests, cultivate their aesthetic sensibilities, or enlarge their

---

[10]The work of Ayn Rand is an exception. But it is unfortunately flawed by a systematic failure to distinguish between outright selfishness and morally appropriate self-regard. For Rand begins by *advocating* selfishness but follows this up by *defending* rational self-interest.

cultural horizons.[11] The self-realization sector of moral philosophy is the missing link of Anglo-American academic ethics at this historical juncture. (Perhaps we have become too democratic to feel comfortable with the elitist mien of an emphasis on personal cultivation.)

This tendency to confine morality to its social, other-oriented dimension, once well established, makes it difficult if not impossible for us to understand and appreciate the thought of those who do not succumb to the narrowed moral vision of the post-utilitarian Anglo-Saxon moral theorists. The recent moral philosophers of Spain are a case in point.

The Spanish Tradition

The Spanish philosophical tradition of moral thought from Balthasar Gracián in the seventeenth century to José Ortega y Gasset in ours has in fact been far more preoccupied with self-realization than with benevolence. Because of Spain's self-imposed intellectual separation from the rest of Western Europe, the scientific revolution and consequent Enlightenment made only a limited cultural impact, and Spanish thought has continued throughout to be pervaded by the deep concern for human things and human values that typified the Renaissance. In Spain, the natural scientist's preoccupation with nature has never quite supplanted the classical humanist's concern for man and his works. Individual pride and an emphatic (and sometimes quixotic) concern for high personal standards have generally been characteristic features of Iberian society.

Take, for example, modern Spain's most eminent philosopher, Miguel de Unamuno (1864–1936).[12] Of Basque origins, and initially trained as a classical scholar at the University of Madrid, he became Professor of Greek at the University of Salamanca in 1891; he continued to serve there for many years also

[11] Least open to this line of complaint is Christina Hoff Sommers, *Vice and Virtue in Everyday Life: Introductory Readings in Ethics*, an anthology of over 60 selections in the normative ethics of individual agents. Still, only some 10 percent of these discussions deal with some aspect of self-development—principally self-respect—and none do so in a significantly concrete way, since in most cases it is abstract theory that is on the author's mind.

[12] For a compact but informative introduction to Unamuno, see the article by Peter Koestenbaum in *The Encyclopedia of Philosophy* (New York, 1967), 8: 182–85.

as Professor of Philosophy. Exiled to the Canary Islands in 1924 for his opposition to Primo de Rivera, he returned to the university with the establishment of the Republic, to occupy the chair of History of the Spanish Language. From 1931 to 1933, he served in the Cortes (Parliament), and in 1934 he was designated Rector for Life at Salamanca. He lived to see the outbreak of civil war in 1935 and came to feel that neither side was working for the best interests of Spain—or of humanity at large.

In his student years, Unamuno was attracted to the "scientific" philosophizing of Auguste Comte and Herbert Spencer—to positivism and naturalism. But he soon transferred his allegiance to Hegelian philosophy and in particular the Hegelian conception of *dialectic*, becoming a practitioner of what he called "the art of paradox," and dwelling on the dualistic complexity of divided allegiances as inherent in the human condition.

Throughout his many productive years, Unamuno was particularly concerned to argue the shortcomings of a one-sidedly scientific/rationalistic approach to human problems. He granted that the findings of science were impressive in their own realm—and in many ways enormously beneficial to man, for example, in medicine. But he saw them as being seriously inadequate and unsatisfactory as a guide to the understanding of man, and the conduct of a satisfying life. In his classic 1913 book *Del sentimiento trágico de la vida*, Unamuno maintained that inquiring reason was incapable of delivering into our hands a world picture with which thinking people can be content because of science's inability to get a purchase on the condition of human life as actually experienced "from within," so to speak. In his view, any attempt to characterize people in scientific terms and categories succeeds only in dehumanizing them, stripping them of their characteristically human personal traits. The salient values of the scientific approach are regularity, lawfulness, consistency, order. And these virtues of scientific rationality are ill-suited to the human condition. In particular, the view of a man that comes from the biological and social sciences is one that we cannot sensibly apply in dealing with our fellows. Accordingly, Unamuno argues passionately against bringing children up on "scientific" lines—particularly in his interesting novel, *Amor y pedagogía* (1902). He constantly stresses the need in all our dealings with people to recognize them—and ourselves—as thoroughly imperfect creatures of flesh and blood. Man is not a rational animal, but a mass of contradictions. It is not intellect and reason, but feeling and sensibility, that lie at the core of human nature. Like Fredrick Hayek later on, Unamuno trusts the glacial pressures toward adequacy of the historical course of experiential developments more than the scientific rationality of man.

Much of Unamuno's work thus consists in a polemic against a "scientific," rationalistic, statistical approach to human beings. To approach human life via the categories and concepts of scientific reason denudes human life of all that conduces to its characteristic savor; in abandoning spontaneity, immediacy, contingency, it loses all that makes life worthwhile. The consequence is a sense of worthlessness that leads to alienation and even suicide. Unamuno is not an irrationalist, not an enemy of reason, but rather a realist who calls into question the ability of the rational side of man by itself to furnish all the guidance needed in the pursuit of the human good. As he sees it, the situation is one of paradox. For us humans, reason is like a very difficult but indispensable mate—we cannot live with it and we cannot live without it.

Unamuno's mode of exposition is true to his skeptical convictions, his method being not so much to endorse a view of human *nature* as to project a view of the human *condition*—the stark realities that confront us in this vale of tears. For life is a *shipwreck*. The actual human situation in this world calls for a deeply pessimistic appraisal. Things do not go "according to plan"; our best efforts are generally frustrated, our fondest hopes disappointed. Unamuno accordingly proceeds not by explaining concepts or articulating theories, but by evoking responses at the level of feelings and sentiments by bringing a certain sort of sensibility to literary expression. He offers a deliberately belletristic rather than scholastic/systematic development of his ideas, proceeding in the same rhetorical mode of exposition that one finds in "existentialist" thinkers like Pascal, Kierkegaard, and Nietzsche. He seeks to form attitudes rather than opinions and to *convert* by addressing a person's entire spirit, rather than simply to *convince* by addressing the intellect alone.

In *Del sentimiento trágico*, Unamuno dwells on man's irrepressible demand—and need—for transcendence. He maintains that we persist in asking more of life than it can possibly deliver. We stake a demand for absoluteness. "Either all or nothing—if man is not everything, he is nothing." Our inner being is pervaded by an unquenchable yearning for a vindication of the value of human existence. But this insistent demand of the human spirit contrasts starkly with the realities of the human condition. The problems of human life admit of no solutions; they can certainly not be addressed effectively by rational planning and cognitive manipulation. In this imperfect world, we simply have to do what we can to make the best of a bad job. A willingness to muddle through by the use of natural instinct and native wit is the better part of human wisdom. On the whole, it is pointless and an open invitation to frustration to use scientific reason as a battering ram to pound out solutions to problems we would be better advised to address with custom or common sense. The sagacious among us endeavor as best they can with the limited means available to infuse their lives with value, realizing all the while that this is a struggle that can never be brought to a satisfactory conclusion.[13]

Deficient and imperfect though we individual humans inevitably are, Unamuno insists on the inherent worth and dignity of the human being. Kant wants us to honor the generic humanity in others; Unamuno, by contrast, insists that we value their idiosyncratic personality, their characteristic individuality. He thoroughly deplores the tendency of modern man to discount the individual in the interests of advancing a cause. Unamuno's dislike of mass movements like communism and fascism roots in his disapproval of their unconcern for the value of the individual. Those who would subordinate the interests of individuals to the pursuit of a grand collective design attract his scorn. Unamuno wants us to focus on the improvement of ourselves as individuals rather than the improvement of statistics. His message is: "If you concern yourself for the good of individual people—yourself prominently included—the 'condition of mankind' will take care of itself." Unamuno's model individual is less preoccupied with social amelioration than with personal development. He counts on personal striving rather than social engineering to help people achieve satisfying lives.

[13] Many of these views are further elaborated in the work of José Ortega y Gasset.

As this example serves to indicate, it becomes difficult for contemporary Anglo-Saxons to appreciate the moralistic tradition of modern Spanish philosophy. To most of us, the Iberians seem to be embarked on a venture of elitist moralism and schoolmasterly exhortation rather than one of serious moral theorizing. The idea that they, rather than ourselves, are faithful to the central core of the Greek heritage of moral philosophy—as indeed they are—strikes us as shocking and perhaps regrettable.[14]

The Need for Balance

A common rationale connects the two hemispheres of moral philosophy, benevolence and self-development. Acting with due concern for the best interests of others and acting with due concern for one's own best interests are both appropriate constituent aspects of caring for the best interests of people in general. The basic idea is that personhood is sacred, and that we are duty-bound—to ourselves, to our fellows, and to the forces that have brought us into being in this world—to care for and foster the interests of personhood wherever we encounter it, be it in others or in ourselves.

Regrettably, moral philosophers have in recent times been reluctant to approach their discipline in a holistic spirit. They have inclined to give exaggerated weight to one part of their overall domain and to downgrade the other. In Spain, there has been an overemphasis on what we have here designated as self-development. In the Anglo-American orbit, by contrast, benevolence-morality has received disproportionate attention. The sensible approach, surely, would be to return moral philosophy to its Greek roots and take a synoptic and holistic view, addressing the issue of a valid moral economy of life overall, in its unified totality.

For there is an important issue of balance here. A pure self-realization doctrine tends to overemphasize the value of devel-

[14]To be sure, the Greek view of the human good as inherent in the nature of the species and the modern ("Protestant") conception of a more highly personalized good make for an important difference in approach. But this difference—important as it is—does not affect the present point that concern for one's own good is an element of morality broadly (and properly) understood.

oping our own talents to the exclusion of giving aid and comfort to others, whereas a pure benevolence ethic tends to overemphasize the value of doing the right thing by others to the detriment of the individual's own growth and development. One can, after all, manage to act properly toward others and nevertheless fail badly to honor the just demands of one's own self-development, being outwardly good yet inwardly stunted. And this too is a serious moral failing. Benevolence exhausts neither the whole range of the human good nor that of morality itself. The issue of self-rationalization is morally inescapable, and has been part and parcel of the domain since its inception.

No doubt, the appropriate systemic balance between these prime desiderata of care for self and care for community will in some degree vary with an individual's own natural makeup and situation. But a morally well-ordered life calls for a fusion of sorts—one where both due care for others and due care for one's own self-development are somehow brought into appropriate balance within an overarchingly unified framework. Providing sensible guidance for how we should go about achieving this end is undeniably a difficult and challenging issue—one that the moral philosophers of classical antiquity raised but certainly did not resolve, and that, as we have seen, their modern-day successors have largely ignored.

Optimism and Pessimism

THE QUARREL between optimism and pessimism has been raging since classical antiquity. Following the lead of the Socrates of Plato's *Timaeus*, the Stoics taught that the world's arrangements are designed for the best and promote the good of all.[1] The followers of Hegesias, on the other hand, maintained that nature is intractable and so operates as to make the achievement of well-being (*eudaimonia*) impossible for man.[2] The two conflicting tendencies have opposed each other since the dawn of philosophical thought.

Optimism

Optimism pivots on the contention that things are well with the world as is, that the arrangements of this world are on balance for the good. But such a general view can take very different specific forms, depending on whether it is maintained that the condition of things is (1) *presently* in good order; or (2) *tending* toward the good, that in the natural course of events, matters will ongoingly assume a better condition; or (3) *moveable* toward the good, that matters can be impelled in this direction, provided only that we do the right things to bring this about. Three different questions are at issue: how things *are*, whither they

---

[1] For a compact account of the Stoic position, see P. P. Hallie, "Stoicism," in *The Encyclopedia of Philosophy* (New York, 1967), 8: 18–22. On the Stoic metaphysics of nature, see S. Sambursky, *Physics of the Stoics* (New York, 1959).

[2] Diogenes Laertius, *Lives of the Philosophers*, 2, sec. 94.

tend, and what *opportunities* are open. When these questions are answered favorably, we may call the three resultant positions *actuality* optimism, *tendency* optimism, and *prospect* optimism, respectively.

Actuality optimism takes the position that things are in good condition as they stand—that, on the whole, all is right with the world in the prevailing order of things. Such a view is usually (but not necessarily) bound up with a commitment to the benevolence of a presiding deity. This view was already voiced by Plato, who maintained that "since He judged that order was in every way for the better, God brought it [the world] from disorder into order."[3]

Tendency optimism, also called *meliorism*, is very different from actuality optimism. It does not necessarily hold that all is well with things as they stand; it simply takes the stance that things are getting better. It compares the present with the future and envisions an improvement in the confident conviction that, whatever might be happening now, better times lie ahead. (However, since improvement is the key issue, the change could in principle merely be from terrible to bad, rather than from good to even better.)

Prospect optimism compares the present as it stands with the prospective future that our efforts and opportunities put at our disposal. It looks to the *presumably realizable* future and maintains that suitable actions on our part can pave the way to improvement. (Not surprisingly, the belief that things will deteriorate despite our best efforts to the contrary represents a prospect pessimism.) Both meliorism (tendency optimism) and prospect optimism are oriented toward the future. But tendency optimism holds that matters *will* get better, while prospect optimism holds that they *can* get better if only we manage to do the right things.

Optimism in all its forms is indissolubly linked to the dimension of value. All the various modes of optimism are *evaluative* positions that contemplate some manner of goodness:

Actuality optimism: things *are* in good condition.
Tendency optimism: things *are moving* toward the better.
Prospect optimism: things *are moveable* toward the better.

[3] *Timaeus*, 30A.

Optimism as we are considering it here is a general evaluative position about "the state of things" at large. Of course, people also speak of "being optimistic" about the favorable outcome of a *particular* situation or episode—the expectation that all will turn out well in, say, the marriage of John and Mary. Our present concern, however, is with *optimism* at the level of generality, rather than with such episodic expectations with respect to individual outcomes. The single-case "optimism" of the gambler who, presumably in the face of considerable counterevidence, thinks that he is bound to win *this* time, or of the drunkard who thinks that *this* bottle will engender no unfortunate results, lies outside the range of the present discussion.

Parameters of Optimism

Four questions can be always raised with respect to any sort of optimism:

What things are being held to be good/improving/improvable?
What manner of "goodness" is at issue: *in what way* is something to be good or better?
Just *how* good or *how much* better?
Good or better *for whom*?

These four questions reflect, respectively, the *range, the mode*, the *degree*, and the envisioned *beneficiaries* of the optimism at issue. By varying these factors, we can obtain, for example, such melioristic theses as "The life expectancy of infants is getting somewhat longer," "Hospital patients are receiving ever more effective care," and "The quality of life is improving for citizens of technically advanced societies."[4]

Different kinds of optimism thus arise from variation in the four parameters. With respect to range and mode this is clear enough. The issue of beneficiaries in particular opens up much scope. We have the prospect that those at issue are:

me = oneself (egocentric optimism);
we = our group (parochial optimism);
many or most people (general optimism);
everyone (universal optimism).

[4] A *technological* optimism to the effect that modern science and technology will create the conditions of a new social order has been very popular in the

The relative inclusiveness of the group of contemplated beneficiaries will determine the scope or scale of the optimism at issue. Of course, the fact that we ourselves can plausibly see improved conditions in the light of *optimism* will hinge crucially on our stance toward the group of beneficiaries—in particular on the question of whether we can identify with them in taking their interests to heart. If the beneficiaries are going to be people whom we wish ill, the prospect of improvement in their lot would hardly represent an optimistic view.

The degree-oriented question *"How much good or better?"* also leads to considerable variation. Consider the evaluation scale:

G*	as good as can be
G+	very good
G	good
O	indifferent
B	bad
B−	very bad
B*	as bad as can be

Given such a spectrum, there are bound to be substantially different varieties of optimism—and, in particular, very different sorts of meliorism. A movement from G to G* is one thing, one from B* to B quite another. It is tempting to think that optimism is a matter of going "from good to better," and pessimism one of going "from bad to worse." But this is a grave oversimplification that takes one prominent case as representative of the whole.

Again, optimism is sometimes characterized as the view that "good will ultimately prevail over evil." But this too is a very special form of the doctrine. Consider a society populated by three groups of people, whose condition is viewed by a certain theory as subject to the course of change set out in Table 8. This theory is surely optimistic, since things are getting better for all three groups. All the same, we do not have a condition where the good ultimately predominates: in the end, the various groups still occupy a condition substantially less than good.

Soviet Union under the influence of Friedrich Engels. See Boris G. Kuznetsov, *Philosophy of Optimism* (Moscow, 1977), which despite its title offers little of philosophical substance.

TABLE 8

Hypothetical Course of Improvement
for Three Groups in the Same Society

Group	Average initial condition	Average final condition
1	B	O
2	B−	B
3	B*	B−

SCALE: O, neutral; B, bad; B−, very bad; B*, as bad as can be.

Different Constructions of Actuality Optimism

Let us consider actuality optimism somewhat more closely. Markedly diverse versions result with varying positions on the standing of the bad—that is, one's view of *the status of negativity* will engender very different results:

1. *Absolute optimism.* Everything is literally for the best. All negativity is only *seemingly* such. Anything bad is, even at worst, only a lack of perfection—a shortfall of the good. Negativity (badness, evil) is nothing substantial as such; everything there is is good, though perhaps in varying degrees.

2. *Instrumental optimism.* There is actual evil and negativity, but whenever present, it serves as a causal means to a greater good. There is always a chain of causes and effects through which any evil is ultimately productive of a predominating good. All those clouds have silver linings: any item of negativity is in fact a causally productive means operating toward augmenting the good. The bads of the world are causally necessary conditions for the realization of greater goods.

3. *Compensatory optimism.* There indeed is evil and negativity. And it is not always causally productive of a predominating good—not in every case simply a means causally conducive to a greater good in just exactly that same causal locality. But at the overall, collective level, the good outweighs the bad. The world is a systemic whole of interlocking elements, and matters are so arranged that a preponderant good always *compensates* for the presence of evil. The good and the bad stand in a relationship of *systemic interconnection*: evil is an integral and irremovable part of a holistic world order that embodies a greater good.

Quite different things are at issue here. With (1) we have a "blind" optimism that refuses to see negativity as something real. With (2) we have a theory of *causal facilitation* that acknowledges the reality of negativity but sees it as a means to greater good. With (3) we have a theory of *compensation* that sees negativity outweighed by a coordinated positivity in the world's overall systemic arrangements.

Some historical observations are in order. It would seem that (1) has not been squarely held by any (Western) philosopher since the neo-Platonism of classical antiquity—mystics and spiritualists aside.[5] The position is clearly at odds with the usual Christian view of the Fall of Man, and to find its more common expression, we must turn to the Oriental religions, which see the phenomenal world with all its evils as *maya*, or illusion. Voltaire's Dr. Pangloss, who sometimes talks in the manner of (1), comes closer to holding (2). But Leibniz, who sometimes talks in the instrumentalist manner of (2) in his *Theodicy*, actually holds the compensatory version at issue in (3). Accordingly, Voltaire's parody of the bad-will-lead-to-good idea in *Candide* does not really hit its target, Leibniz.

A theory that denies the existence of the bad only because it *also* denies the existence of good within the context of a comprehensive denial of *all* value in the world's arrangements—in short, a Spinozistic negation of objective value—cannot be called a form of optimism. It falls outside the optimism–pessimism spectrum and is at odds with it.

Tendency Optimism (Meliorism or Progressivism)

Tendency optimism is not a single theory but a madding crowd of theories of the most diverse kinds, with little in common save their generic structure: things of some sort are getting better in some way or other for certain beneficiaries. In particular, when these beneficiaries are people in general, then a melioristic position represents a doctrine that sees the world's arrangements as fundamentally favorable to the interests of man.

Meliorism in all its versions constitutes a *substantive* doctrine about the nature of the world and its course of events. Once a

[5] Mary Baker Eddy wrote that "evil is but an illusion, and it has no real basis. Evil is a false belief." *Science and Health* (Boston, 1934), p. 480, secs. 23–24.

standard of good and bad is given, it represents a factual thesis to the effect that a course of change of a certain sort is under way and is, accordingly, matter-of-factly true or false. This is illustrated by what is perhaps the most usual and familiar form of meliorism, the version based on the following parameters:

Range: conditions of life ("quality of life");
Mode: qualitative improvement;
Degree: from bad (B) to very good (G+);
Beneficiaries: mankind at large.

The resulting melioristic thesis maintains that the quality of life is getting ever-better for people at large and is moving toward a generally good condition. Once we are informed about how this matter of "quality of life" is to be assessed, the thesis becomes a straightforward factual one that turns on how matters actually stand on the world's stage.

But while such a melioristic view is clearly factual in character, the fact at issue is patently an *evaluative* fact. Meliorative optimism stakes a claim that can be understood (and substantiated) only relative to a suitable standard of value to provide the necessary yardstick of evaluation. It is a substantive doctrine that is predicated on an essentially normative basis.

With any mode of meliorism, the question of the *pace* of improvement will always arise. When things are held to be getting better and better, the issue of velocity looms—a snail's pace vs. an avalanche-like rush. Moreover, any meliorism that looks to a coming improvement leaves open the question of just *when* this transformation will come about—whether soon or in the impenetrable fog of a future "eventually." If we look optimistically with Peirce to a cognitive victory of science over nature or with Marx to the political triumph of proletarian power, there yet remains the crucial issue of just when this happy eventuation is to be realized. With eschatological meliorism, as with doomsday theologies, the all-important question of timing is always there.

Meliorism is indissolubly linked to the idea of *progress*: any theory of progress is a mode of meliorism, and, conversely, any meliorism a progressivism. For progress necessarily involves something more than mere *change*, namely, *improvement*, since progress is change in some positively evaluated direction, encompassing a sequence of events in whose course things are "getting better" in some fashion or other. Accordingly, there will be as many distinct types of meliorism as there are types of progress. Very different sorts of "courses of ongoing improvement" can be contemplated: material, intellectual, social, moral, and the like. The complexity and diversity of meliorism come to the fore in this connection. The same range of questions that apply to meliorism in general will apply to a progressivism of any sort: how fast, how far, how distributed, etc.

The distributional aspects of meliorism are of particular interest. Suppose a scale from 0–100, a *hedonic* scale, say, or a scale of *quality of life*, or some such—the details do not matter so long as we are operating in a context where "bigger is better." Consider now two very different cases:

Case 1. The *average* gets bigger and bigger, but the *minimum* gets ever less.
Year 1: 90% of the time at 90, 10% at 20
Year 2: 90% of the time at 95, 10% at 10
Year n: 90% of the time at halfway between the preceding year's 90% value and 100; 10% of the time at halfway between the preceding year's 10% value and 0.

Case 2. The *average* gets less and less, but the *minimum* gets ever bigger.
Year 1: 90% of the time at 90, 10% at 10
Year 2: 90% of the time at 70, 10% at 20
Year n: 90% of the time at halfway between the preceding year's 90% value and 50; 10% of the time at halfway between the preceding year's 10% value and 30.

These examples show that we will get very different sorts of "course of ever-continuing improvement," depending on whether we focus on the situation *on the average* or on the situation *at the minimum*.[6] There is accordingly a substantial prospect for disagreement and controversy with regard to just this question, "Does improvement in a particular respect actually consti-

[6] Recall the comparably problematic position of John Rawls's *Theory of Justice* (Cambridge, Mass., 1971) that the demands of justice focus on the condition of those at the very bottom of the scale.

tute an improvement on the whole?" With melioristic optimism, it may not be all that clear exactly what sorts of "course of improvement" should actually count as a *meaningful* or *significant* improvement.

It is illuminating to consider the historical example of Leibniz in this connection. Leibnizian optimism is a complex and many-sided theory—a combination of several distinct forms of optimism. It involves, as we have seen, an endorsement of the compensatory version of actuality optimism. But another important feature is the contention that this world of ours is "the best possible world"—with stress on *possible*. There is, no doubt, a good deal that is not right with the world, but all the attainable alternatives are even worse. (Voltaire's ironic plaint, "If this is the best of all possible worlds, what, then, of the others?," implements rather than invalidates the Leibnizian approach.) Leibniz was not one of those rosy-visioned theologians who argue that all of the world's evils and imperfections are mere illusions— that if only we saw things more fully and deeply, we would come to realize our mistake and reclassify all those negativities as goods. As they see it, all imperfection is only *seeming* imperfection—evils are simply shadows needed to secure the painting's overall effectiveness, and any complaint about the badness of things reflects a misunderstanding arising from an *incomplete* understanding.[7] But this possible (albeit problematic) line of absolutist optimism just is not Leibniz's. Leibniz was quite prepared to recognize that much is wrong in the world. But all the other possibilities are worse (even a half-full barrel can be fuller than all the rest). Leibniz recognized evil as real. But he saw it as a systemically necessary condition for the greater good. The myth of Sextus at the end of the *Theodicy* illustrates this: "The crime of Sextus serves for great things: It renders Rome free; thence will arise a great empire, which will show noble examples to mankind."[8] The world's arrangements are systemically interconnected. If we improved something here, even more would come unstruck over there—an "improvement" at

[7] This is essentially the doctrine of Plotinus: all existence roots in the divine One and is therefore good; evil is not something positive and real as such, but only something negative, a mere lack or deficiency of good. See especially *Enneads*, III, ii, 3–18; IV, iii, 13–18; IV, iv, 45.

[8] G. W. Leibniz, *Theodicy*, sec. 416.

one point of the system always has damaging repercussions at another.[9] (As with the harmony of a painting, however, the connections are matters of harmonization and systemic inter-linkage, not of causal interaction.)

A further aspect of Leibnizian optimism is a meliorism with respect to the conditions of life for organic creatures in general and rational beings in particular. Of course, this is not to say that these conditions are superbly good or (given the inherent imper-fections of finite creatures) that they can ever become so. But things will improve on balance in the long run.

The salient feature of Leibniz's position remains in its commit-ment to a compensatory optimism that sees the world as good on the whole. It is *now and always* the case that, on balance, con-sidering everything, the good outweighs the bad even here and now. Via the Christian neo-Platonism of thinkers like Augustine and Aquinas, Leibniz is deeply committed to the idea of a cos-mic order that is essentially good. Good predominates over evil at every stage of the world's history. Leibniz sees this as essen-tial to regarding the world as the creation of a benevolent deity. In *this* regard, Schopenhauer's pessimism is a flat-out denial of Leibnizian optimism. Unlike Voltaire, Schopenhauer identifies his target correctly. In any case, the example of Leibniz shows that a meliorism of the tendency-optimism variety is perfectly compatible with the endorsement of an actuality optimism. The world's improvability need not be seen as conflicting with the idea that it is good as is.

Given this combination of views, there is no doubt that Leib-niz's position is properly characterized as a version of opti-mism. But it is certainly not one of the facile ostrich-head-in-the-ground sort, which maintains that everything is just fine and dandy, seeing no evil simply because it refuses, in Pollyanna-ish fashion, to look evil in the face.

Is meliorism tenable at all? Memento mori. Does not the inev-itability of death automatically preclude any possibility of being

---

[9]Catherine Wilson writes: "It is of course common knowledge that Leibniz believed that the appearance of evil in the world was only a symptom of our defective or limited understanding." "Leibnizian Optimism," *Journal of Philoso-phy*, 80 (1983): 767. But "common knowledge" is quite wrong here. Leibniz holds not that evil in the world is mere appearance but rather that it is compensated for by a preponderant good.

optimistic about the condition of man? Presumably not. The inexorability of death does indeed preclude the possibility of ever-continuing improvement at the individual level. But the general condition of the continuing group (clan, nation, species) may well improve, despite the merely transient presence of its particular members. ("I myself grow older," Caesar lamented, "yet the crowd in the Appian Way ever remains the same age.") Thus only egocentric people who are concerned for themselves alone are denied a recourse to optimism. Those whose wider range of concern embraces their posterity at large can in principle be optimistic about the human condition—ignoring for the moment such remote eventualities as the "heat death" of the solar system.

On the other hand, it would seem that mainstream Christianity is at odds with an unalloyed optimism regarding the condition of man as such. The kingdom it contemplates is not of this world, and it is not through our own powers and abilities that we humans can come to enter it. The progressivist theory of the perfectability of man through the ministrations of science is a modern notion, the work of theorists of the Age of Enlightenment seeking to supplant an older, less sanguine view of human prospects here on earth.

In any case, the melioristic thesis that things are tending toward the better is generally difficult to establish. The best we can standardly claim on *evidential* grounds is that things are getting better *at present*. And this seldom affords a firm guarantee for the future. (Our most secure inductive conclusion is that the long-term projection of current tendencies is generally inappropriate.)

The fact that meliorism is hard to substantiate has its other side in the fact that it is also hard to refute. Even if things have not gone well of late, this may well be a matter of preparation for a strong spurt toward the better: *reculer pour mieux sauter*. Sometimes one must travel east to go west—via the Panama Canal, for example. Appearances can be deceiving; the circumstance that things do not look to be getting better does not really mean they are not. The fact that melioristic optimism is hard to refute on evidential grounds opens the door to contemplating its acceptance on a nonevidential basis through a pragmatic rather than probative route to validation. This idea has important ramifications.

Attitudinal Optimism

Optimism as we have so far considered it is a *substantive* and *descriptive* (albeit value-determined) position. But there is room for yet another version—an optimism whose character is *attitudinal* rather than strictly *descriptive*. It is represented by a policy of proceeding (when possible) in the confident hope that the tendency or prospect afforded by the future is auspicious—that things will work out well, and matters continue to improve. Such attitudinal optimism is something very different from the descriptively fact-oriented modes of optimism with which we have dealt so far. It does not presuppose the actuality of a meliorative tendency or prospect. Rather, it is an attitudinal disposition toward viewing things in a favorable light as a basis for action. Attitudinal optimism is not a matter of a cognitively well-based conviction about how things will comport themselves in the world, but represents a praxis-geared posture of hopeful confidence. What is at issue is not a well-evidentiated *thesis* but a *hopeful attitude* one takes toward the future when this is not precluded by the state of one's information. The assumption of such a position accordingly does not involve any actual *prediction* that the contemplated course of improvement will eventuate, but only a *confidently hopeful anticipation* that this will occur; what is at issue is a point of practical policy rather than one of factual foreknowledge.

Consider an illustration. Hegel was an optimist, and both the Hegelian left and the Hegelian right share the fundamental optimism of their master, but in very different ways. On the left lies the tendency optimism represented by the eschatological posture of dialectical materialism—a melioristic view predicated on the historical inevitability of a better order of things (for the proletariat at any rate). And on the right lies the attitudinal optimism of the German idealists—a position that is not comparably eschatological, but represents an optimism of attitude and intellectual orientation rather than historical process. The former is an essentially predictive position, the latter an essentially attitudinal one.

Many expressions of attitudinal optimism are of course to be found in the pragmatic philosophy of William James, but its main theoretical exponent was the obscure Austrian philosopher Hieronymus Lorm.[10] With an eye on Kant's distinction between a phenomenal and a noumenal order, Lorm contrasts the order of experience (*Erfahrung*) with the order of sensibility (*Empfindung*). The bitter lessons of experience endorse pessimism, but the positive inclination of human sensibility calls for a life-enhancing optimism. Lorm accordingly endorses an attitudinal optimism (*Meinungs-Optimismus*) that is evidentially "groundless," because it flies in the face of our actual experience of how the world actually goes (our *Erfahrungs-Pessimismus*). But it is nevertheless seen as valid—experience to the contrary notwithstanding—as an expression of the inner spirit of man. Somewhat as in Kant, we are dual citizens belonging both to an empirical realm where optimism is inappropriate and to a noumenal realm where optimism is mandatory.

Attitudinal optimism is thus a matter of outlook and perception—of attitude or disposition rather than expectation and belief. The tendency optimist counsels *patience*: "Wait! Things will get better." The attitudinal optimist counsels *confidence*: "Hope! Don't let your spirit be crushed by present adversity. Spirit is something too valuable to be diminished by events whose overall worth in the larger scheme of things isn't all that big." Attitudinal optimism accordingly represents a fundamentally *evaluative* rather than a factually *predictive* posture.

Validating Attitudinal Optimism

But can these positions of personal *attitude* and factual *belief* be kept apart? Does attitudinal optimism not somehow require the support of melioristic convictions and thus require a grounding in scientific foreknowledge?

Not at all. It is perfectly possible for someone to adopt an optimistic attitude—quite reasonably and rationally—without being convinced of the factual thesis that a substantively optimistic trend or tendency indeed obtains. Even in situations where one cannot substantiate a melioristic tendency, one may well be able to validate an attitudinal optimism—not, to be sure, on evidential grounds but on pragmatic ones. One can, that is,

[10] See Hieronymus Lorm, *Der grundlose Optimismus: Ein Buch der Betrachtung* (Vienna, 1894). Friedrich Ueberweg, *Grundriss der Geschichte der Philosophie* 12th ed. (Berlin, 1923), part 4, provides some information about Lorm.

validate attitudinal optimism by maintaining (1) that factually *nihil obstat*, that the available evidence does not stand decisively in its way, and (2) that positive consequences will (or are likely to) follow on one's proceeding in a hope-and-expectation of optimistic tenor. These considerations yield a pragmatic rather than evidential justification—a justification on the basis of *consequences* rather than *grounds*. Accordingly, I can (quite reasonably) proceed to plan and conduct my actions in the firm hope that a favorable course of developments will unfold without first determining that this is actually (or indeed even probably) the case.

The principle at issue here is not that of the precept, "Proceed in good hope and you will (certainly or at least very likely) succeed," nor yet that of the precept, "Proceed in good hope since you have nothing to lose thereby," but rather that of the precept, "Proceed in good hope and you will improve the chances of success." If a policy for guiding one's actions can make even a small positive contribution to the probability that a desirable state of affairs will be realized, then its adoption can make good rational sense. When the balance of potential advantage is favorably adjusted, then those hopeful expectations are rationally defensible—albeit in the pragmatic rather than evidential mode of rationality.[11]

Yet how is one to reply to the objector who says: "Attitudinal optimism is not rationally justified in the absence of evidential support. In such cases one should not form anticipations at all but simply await developments." The response is straightforward. *Why not* adopt such a posture? Why simply wait with folded hands rather than act in hopeful expectation—particularly if such action can improve the prospects of a favorable outcome?

This decision-theoretic perspective carries us back to the position advocated by William James in *Pragmatism*. As long as I am appropriately convinced that a policy of hopeful action can make a positive difference, attitudinal optimism can make good decision-theoretic sense—even where factual determinations are infeasible. An optimistic attitude can manifest "the power of positive thinking," as in the following example: "In the ordinary

[11]On the issues involved in the contrast between evidential and pragmatic justification, see my book, *Pascal's Wager* (Notre Dame, Ind., 1985).

affairs of life, act (in the absence of evidence to the contrary) as if the people with whom you deal were reliable and honest." It certainly is not true that people in general are trustworthy. The justification of such a "pragmatic belief" can reside in the efficacy of the practical policy that it underwrites—its capacity to engender positive results—and need not call for preestablishing its substantive correctness as a factual thesis. It can, in principle, make perfectly good practical sense to proceed in a spirit of optimism even when the prospects of success are small. When we must play a stronger team, we do well to strive with an effort bolstered by sanguine hope, remembering that with luck even puny David can prevail over mighty Goliath, and that victory is not invariably on the side of the big battalions.

Consider this objection: "Surely it is not rational ever to let our attitudes be shaped in a way that outruns the reaches of our knowledge. To allow our outlook to be influenced by our values is just a matter of inappropriate wishful thinking." This objection hits wide of the mark in its insistence in the name of "rationality" that attitudes must be shaped by *knowledge* alone. Rationality is a matter of the intelligent pursuit of appropriate objectives. And here knowledge does not have it all to itself. Humans not are *purely* cognitive creatures—we do not live by information alone, and knowledge is not our only value. The sphere of our praxis must be allowed to play its part in the overall rational order of things. An optimistic attitude can thus be perfectly "rational" in appropriate circumstances.

The crux is simply this. There are two very different sorts of rationally valid expectations about the future—namely, *cognitively justified anticipations* based on evidence, and *pragmatically justified hopes* based on decision-theoretic considerations. The two can get out of step with one another. But there is nothing at all irrational or unreasonable about this—when the decision-theoretic aspects of the matter are heeded, it makes perfectly good rational sense because quite different things are at issue. Cognitive rationality is not the only sort; practical rationality can also come into operation.

Acting so as to fly in the face of established *facts* is never rationally justified. But acting to fly in the face of mere *probabilities* can on occasion be justifiable. Indeed that is exactly what we standardly do in decision theory when we balance probabilities against prospective gains and losses, placing our bets on the side of the more favorable expectations. We can, quite appropriately, sometimes bet on long shots. Even if I am pessimistic and believe that the chances of realizing the good are low no matter what I do, the fact remains that when these chances are increased by my taking an optimistic attitude, then I am well advised to do so. And this is what matters for practical purposes. Even for a pessimist, an optimistic attitude may well pay off.

To be sure, the advantageousness, and thus the rational advisability, of optimism or pessimism will very much depend on conditions and circumstances. There are certainly situations where optimism is unwarranted and where it is a matter of unrealistically inappropriate wishful thinking that verges on self-deception to persist in thinking that matters will eventuate favorably. It is clearly foolish to be optimistic in cases where a failure to cut one's losses is simply to throw good money after bad; attitudinal optimism would obviously be ill-advised here. The sensible thing is to control our attitudes by a rational analysis of the objective situation, including a realistic appraisal of the likelihood of both the possible outcomes and their potential costs and benefits. The course of wisdom is a guarded optimism, tempered by a realistic appreciation of the determinable facts.

The rational optimist is accordingly one who adopts this policy not as a *general rule* but as a *working presumption*: "In the absence of sufficiently powerful indications to the contrary, act in the confident hope that your efforts will prove to good avail." (What is at issue is a presumption on the same order as that which underlies trusting other people and believing what they say.) The sensible thing is not to be optimistic always and everywhere, in season and out of season, but to be discriminating and allow the characteristics of particular cases and circumstances their just due. From the rational point of view, attitudinal optimism is a policy whose appropriateness is distinctly limited— and yet, within its proper limits, it has its place.

Pessimism and Other Alternatives

Much of what has here been said about optimism has its counterpart on the other side of the coin, the side of pessimism.

In particular, *pejorism* is the reverse of meliorism, embodied in the claim that things are getting worse and worse. As such, it is not necessarily a matter of gloom and doom. In theory, the deterioration at issue may simply take us from superb to excellent.

Schopenhauerian pessimism, on the other hand, is the doctrine that, on balance, the evils of this world outweigh the benefits—that the condition of sentient beings in general and intelligent beings in particular is such that pain exceeds pleasure, and suffering outweighs happiness.[12] As Schopenhauer put it in characteristically picturesque language: "If you try to imagine, as nearly as you can, how much of misery, pain, and suffering of every kind the sun shines upon in its course, you will admit that it would be much better if the sun had been as little able to call forth the phenomenon of life here on the earth as on the moon, and if here, as there, the surface were still in a crystalline state."[13] Even in such a view, however, it does not necessarily follow that it would be better if the world did not exist at all. For it is possible to take the line that benefits in the nonaffective range (including, for example, knowledge or personal goodness) could redeem a negativity of conditions in specifically affective regards—that suffering is the price we pay for the realization of some other values, such as wisdom or loving-kindness, and that it is worth it.

The fact that there are many different modes of optimism and pessimism means that it is possible to combine versions of the one with versions of the other. An interesting example is provided in the curious synthesis of Hegel and Schopenhauer (strange bedfellows!) found in Eduard von Hartmann's *Philosophie des Unbewussten* (1869). Von Hartmann holds, with Hegel, that there is indeed a spiritual dialectical progress in the evolution of consciousness and thought. But he also maintains, with Schopenhauer, that this is achieved at so great a cost in misery and suffering that it would be better if the world did not exist at all. Similarly, Friedrich Engels was inspired by Malthus and Darwin to think of world history as the sphere of operation of a

---

[12] Schopenhauer, of course, did not invent this view. It was already urged against Leibniz by Voltaire (in *Candide*), by Maupertuis (*Oeuvres*, Paris, 1756, 1: 202–5), and by Kant.

[13] "Nachträge zur Lehre vom Leiden der Welt," sec. 156.

cruel force that exacts the sacrifice of millions of lives for the realization of every step of progress—a view that has doubtless
provided aid and comfort to this century's Communist rulers.[14]

Moreover, optimism and pessimism do not exhaust the field.
There is, of course, also room for a Spinozistic naturalism that
sees the world's course of events as totally indifferent to the affairs of man, inclined neither positively nor negatively toward
matters of human good and evil, and providing a neutral stage-
setting where matters of human well-being or ill-being are nowise programmed into the course of events, but determined
substantially by the subjective reaction of human minds.

In fact, as the following list shows, every possible position in
this domain has been advocated by some thinker or other:

1. Value (good and bad) does not apply to the world at all
(Spinoza, rigid materialism, positivism).
2. Value does indeed apply to the world and does so in such
a way that
   (a) the world is maximally good—as good as it is possible for
   a world to be (Leibniz);
   (b) the world is predominantly (though not maximally) good
   (neo-Platonism);
   (c) the world is a (more or less) evenly balanced mixture of
   good and bad (Manicheanism);
   (d) the world is predominantly (though not maximally) bad
   (Schopenhauer);
   (e) the world is maximally bad (Julius Bahnsen).[15]

As is often the case with philosophical controversies, every fea-
sible alternative has found its exponent. (Of course, to note that
a case has been made for each of these diverse alternatives is not
to say that all are of equal merit.)

[14] John Stuart Mill too wondered whether evolutionary progress was "worth
purchasing by the sufferings and wasted lives of entire geological periods." Mill,
Three Essays on Religion (New York, 1970), pp. 192–93. He eventually came to
abandon the utilitarians' faith in progress and hoped at best for a steady-state
condition in regard to human well-being. See Lewis S. Feuer, "John Stuart Mill
as a Sociologist," in J. M. Robson and M. Laine, eds., *James and John Stuart Mill:
Papers of the Centenary Conference* (Toronto, 1976), pp. 98–99.
[15] On this obscure German philosopher, see "Pessimismus," in Rudolf Eisler,
Handwörterbuch der Philosophie, 2d ed. (Berlin, 1922), pp. 473–74. Bahnsen's principal work is *Der Widerspruch im Wissen und Wesen der Welt*, 2 vols. (Leipzig,

Pessimism Versus Optimism

Pessimism invites despair, optimism confidence. The former looks on the dark side, the latter on the bright. Common sense and "realism" alike require us to recognize both dimensions—holding two opposed factors in some sort of reasonable balance. The question is ultimately one of where we focus, of what aspect of a thoroughly mixed situation deserves to be accented.

Optimism takes a characteristic stance here. It is a policy that goes beyond realism to enclose a principle of hope. It recognizes man as a creature of a Pascalian duality of mind and heart—of a binocular vision that sees with the body's eye what there is and with the mind's eye what there should be. It presses beyond fact to the impetus of value—not by failing to see things as they are, but by looking also toward what there might and should be. As the optimist sees it, the good outweighs the bad not in the balance of actuality but in the balance of importance. Optimists do not shut their eyes to the imperfections of the real, but work in cheerful hopefulness toward the amelioration of those imperfections.

The risk of disappointment is the unavoidable price of attitudinal optimism. If one is erroneously optimistic during a course of deterioration, one is going to find one's hopes dashed, one's expectations disappointed. Pessimism manifests the other side of the coin here. If one is a pessimist during a course of improvement, one is going to be pleasantly surprised when those unhappy apprehensions turn out to be unwarranted. But to say this is not to say that pessimism is a wise policy during times of betterment, for it is bound to lead one to lose out on opportunities. Moreover, pessimists who resort to this "pleasant surprise" line of thought to support their position run into problems. For to justify taking a pessimistic stance on *this* basis—because one expects it to lead to pleasant surprises—is ultimately incoherent

---

1882). His bibliography is given in Ueberweg, *Grundriss der Geschichte der Philosophie*, 4: 341–42, 701. For Bahnsen, the world is so designed as to frustrate every human hope and aspiration, and life is like a game of chance played against a diabolical house that is sure to win in the end. Death is not only the end of life but its *telos* as well. Life affirmation is the worst policy: the more we bet on life, the larger our losses are bound to be. The precept, "seek everywhere and choose the smallest evil, never the greatest good," represents the course of true wisdom (*Der Widerspruch*, 2: 492).

and inconsistent: it predicates pessimism on optimism. (The self-consistent line is for pessimists, expecting deterioration, to support their position on grounds of its averting disappointment.)

Under what sorts of circumstances would an attitudinal pessimism that operates in the expectation that things are getting worse possibly be pragmatically justified as somehow useful or productive? Only if it actually helped us to prepare for the worst, to safeguard ourselves helpfully against difficulties that do indeed lie ahead. Thus attitudinal pessimism might pay off as a practical policy in leading people to take sensible precautions in the face of impeding misfortune. But, of course, this can prove to good avail only if (factually speaking) those pessimistic expectations correctly characterize the objective situation. For pessimism to prove advantageous, the expectation at issue must be *correct*—the deterioration we anticipate must in fact be forthcoming.

In this regard, then, there is an interesting asymmetry between the two positions of attitudinal optimism and attitudinal pessimism. A pessimistic attitude is of advantage only if pessimism is correct as a substantive position and things are indeed going downhill, while an optimistic attitude can also be useful when the reverse of its expectations is the case. The advantage of optimism is that it need not be predictively warranted to be pragmatically useful. Even if it eventuates as not justified in actual historical fact, attitudinal optimism can induce us to make things better than they otherwise would be. This sort of thing cannot happen with attitudinal pessimism.

The optimist hopes; even when things look bleak, he anticipates a happy issue. The pessimist fears; even when there are good prospects of a favorable issue, he anticipates the worst and expects disaster. But fear is almost always a bad counselor. Hope is seldom so (though it *sometimes* can be: the investor who expects a current stock rally to last forever is a fool).

An optimistic attitude impels its owner-operator to act with confidence—to run risks in hopeful expectancy that things will go well. It supports activity and enterprise. A pessimistic attitude tends to immobilize. If one confidently expects the worst, there is little point in doing anything save what can be done in the way of safeguards and insurance. And a sufficiently deep pessimism will dissuade one even from taking such measures, because one expects that even they will prove unavailing. Insofar as these attitudinal matters lie within our control, we do well to favor the optimistic approach. Hope invites the penalty of disappointment but has the benefit of sustaining courage in the face of adversity. Pessimism invites inaction and, even worse, a despair that brings no benefits at all. We prefer optimism to pessimism in our companions because optimism is by its very nature life-enhancing.

The rational impetus to optimism lies in the fact that little is more bleak and more inhumane than a life not nourished by some hope of better things to come—if not for oneself and one's posterity, then for one's successors at large. Concern for our fellows and our species is not altogether unselfish. By taking such a stance, we enlarge our stake in the world's affairs and broaden the basis of the hopefulness that endows our own life and labors with a significance they would otherwise lack. The extinction of hope is the ultimate evil.[16]

[16] This chapter draws on one of the same title in the author's *Ethical Idealism* (Berkeley, Calif., 1987).

THIRTEEN

The Power of Ideals

IDEALS PIVOT about the question, "If I could shape the world in my own way, how would I have it be?" And, of course, *every* voluntary action of ours is in some manner a remaking of the world—at any rate, of a very small corner of it—by projecting into reality a situation that otherwise would not be. To act intelligently is to act with due reference to the *direction* in which our own actions shift the course of things. And this is exactly where ideals come into play. Our ideals guide and consolidate our commitment to human virtues in general and moral excellences in particular. Courage and unselfishness provide examples. Acts of courage or selflessness often go beyond "the call of duty," exhibiting a dimension of morality that transcends the boundaries of obligation in a way that is typical of ideals.

In an influential 1958 paper, the English philosopher J. O. Urmson stressed the ethical importance of the Christian conception of works of supererogation (*opera supererogationis*), reemphasizing the traditional contrast between the *basic* morality of duties and the *higher* morality of preeminently creditable action "above and beyond the call of duty."[1] Such supererogation is best conceived of not in terms of duty but in terms of dedication to an ideal. The values at issue are often symbolized in such role models as heroes and saints. An ethic of ideals can accommo-

---

[1] "Saints and Heroes," in A. I. Melden, ed., *Essays in Moral Philosophy* (Seattle, 1958). On this theme, see also David Heyd, *Supererogation: Its Status in Ethical Theory* (Cambridge, 1984).

date what is at issue here in ways a mere ethic of duty cannot. None of us has a *duty* to our fellows to become a saint or hero; this just is not something we *owe* to people, be it singly or collectively. Such "duty" as there is will be that of the diffuse but nevertheless sometimes compelling "sense of duty" that calls on one to be or become a person of a certain sort. Here we are, strictly speaking, dealing not so much with something owed as with the dedication to an ideal—the inner impetus to do one's utmost to make the world into a certain sort of place, even if only that very small corner of it that consists of oneself.

A knowledge of people's ideals gives us much insight into what they do. "By their ideals shall ye know them." We come to know a great deal about someone when we know about his or her ideals—about the person's dreams, heroes, and utopias. The question of what gods somebody worships—power or fame or Mammon or Jehovah—does much to inform us about the sort of person we are dealing with. (To be sure, what we do not yet know is how *dedicated* this person is to those ideals—how energetically and assiduously he or she puts them to work.)

Human aspiration is not restricted by the realities—neither by the realities of the present moment (from which our sense of future possibilities can free us) nor even by our view of realistic future prospects (from which our sense of the ideal possibilities can free us). Our judgment is not bounded by what *is*, or by what *will* be, or even by what *can* be. For there is always also our view of what *should* be. The vision of our mind's eye extends to circumstances beyond the limits of the possible. A proper appreciation of ideals calls for a recognition of the human being's unique dual citizenship in the worlds of the real and the ideal— a realm of facts and a realm of values.

It is remarkable that nature has managed to evolve a creature who aspires to more than nature can offer, who never totally feels at home in its province, but lives, to some extent, as an alien in a foreign land. All those who feel dissatisfied with the existing scheme of things, who both yearn *and strive* for something better and finer than this world affords, have a touch of moral grandeur in their makeup that deservedly evokes admiration.

Skeptically inclined "realists" have always questioned the significance of ideals on the grounds that, being unrealizable, they are presumably pointless. But this fails to reckon properly with the realities of the situation. For while ideals are, in a way, mere fictions, they nevertheless direct and canalize our thought and action. To be sure, an ideal is not a goal we can expect to attain. But it serves to set a direction in which we can strive. Ideals are irrealities, but they are irrealities that condition the nature of the real through their influence on human thought and action. Stalin's cynical question, "But how many divisions has the Pope?," betokens the Soviet *Realpolitiker* rather than the Marxist ideologue. (How many soldiers did Karl Marx command?) It is folly to underestimate the strength of an attachment to ideals. Though in itself impracticable, an ideal can nevertheless importantly influence our praxis and serve to shape the sort of home we endeavor to make for ourselves in a difficult world.

Ideals take us beyond experience into the realm of *imagination*—outside of what we do find, or expect to find, here in this real world, into the region of wishful thinking, of utopian aspiration, of what we would fain have if only (alas!) we could. Admittedly, this envisions a perfection or completion that outreaches not only what we have actually attained, but even what we can possibly attain in this sublunary dispensation. However, to give this up, to abandon casting periodic wistful glances in the "transcendental" direction is to cease to be fully, genuinely, and authentically human. In following empiricists and positivists by fencing the ideal level of deliberation off behind NO ENTRY signs, we diminish the horizons of human thought to its grave impoverishment. (As is readily illustrated by examples from Galileo to Einstein, there is a valid place for thought-experiments that involve idealization even in the domain of the natural sciences themselves.)

The idealized level of contemplation provides a most valuable conceptual instrument. For it affords us a most useful *contrast conception* that serves to shape and condition our thought. Like the functionary in imperial Rome who stood at the emperor's side to whisper intimations of mortality into his ear, idealizations serve to remind us of the fragmentary, incomplete, and parochial nature of what we actually manage to accomplish. If the ideal level of consideration were not there for purposes of contrast, we would constantly be in danger of ascribing to the parochially proximate a degree of completeness or adequacy to which it has no just claims.

To restrain our thought from operating at the idealized level of a global inclusiveness that transcends the reach of actual experience would create a profound impoverishment of our intellectual resources. To block off our entry into the sphere of perfection represented by the ideal level of consideration is to cut ourselves off from a domain of thought that characterizes us as intellectually amphibious creatures who are able to operate in the realm of realities and ideals.

Expelled from the Garden of Eden, we are cut off from the whole sphere of completeness, perfection, comprehensiveness, and totality. We are constrained to make do with the flawed realities of a mundane and imperfect world. But we aspire to more. Beset by a "divine discontent," we cannot but yearn for that unfettered completeness and perfection that (as empiricists rightly emphasize) the limited resources of our cognitive situation cannot actually afford us. Not content with graspable satisfactions, we seek far more and press outward "beyond the limits of the possible." It is a characteristic *and worthy* feature of our species that our thought reaches out toward a greater completeness and comprehensiveness than anything actually available within the mundane sphere of secured experience. *Homo sapiens* alone among earthly creatures is a being able and (occasionally) willing to work toward the realization of a condition of things that does not and perhaps cannot exist—a state of affairs where values are fully and comprehensively embodied. We are agents who can change and transform the world, striving to produce something that does not exist save in the mind's eye, and indeed cannot actually exist at all because its realization calls for a greater perfection and completeness than the recalcitrant conditions of this world allow. Our commitment to this level of deliberation makes us into a creature that is something more than a rational animal—a creature that moves in the sphere of not only ideas but ideals as well.

The Pragmatic Validation of Ideals

What do ideals do for us? What useful role do they play in the human scheme of things? The answer runs something like this. *Homo sapiens* is a rational agent. People can act and must choose among alternative courses of action. This crucial element of choice means that our actions will be guided in the first instance by considerations of "necessity" relating to survival and physical well-being. But to some extent they can, and in an advanced condition of human development *must*, go far beyond this point. Eventually they come to be guided by necessity-transcending considerations, by our "higher" aspirations—a yearning for a life that is not only secure and pleasant but also *meaningful* in having some element of excellence or nobility about it. Ideals are the guideposts toward these higher, excellence-oriented aspirations. As such, they motivate rather than constrain, urge rather than demand.

The validation of an ideal is ultimately derivative. It does not lie in the (unrealizable) state of affairs that it contemplates—in that inherently unachievable perfection it envisions. Rather, it lies in the influence that it exerts on the lives of its human exponents through the mediation of thought. To be sure, one ideal can be evaluated in terms of another. But to employ our ideological commitments in appraising ideals is ultimately question begging—a matter of appraising values in terms of values. To appraise ideals in a way that avoids begging the question we must leave the domain of idealization altogether and enter into that of the realistically practical. The superiority of one ideal over another must be tested by its *practical consequences* for human well-being. "By their fruits shall ye know them." In appraising ideals, we must look not to the *nature* of these ideals alone but also to their *work*. For the key role of an ideal is to serve as an instrument of decision-making—a sort of navigation instrument for use in the pursuit of the good. And here the homely practical goods—survival, health, well-being, human solidarity, happiness, and the like—come into their own once more. Those higher values validate their legitimacy in terms of their bearing on the quotidian ones.

By urging us to look beyond the limits of the practicable, ideals help us to optimize the efficacy of our praxis. Their significance turns on what we do with them in the world—on their utility in guiding our thought and action into fruitful and rewarding directions, wholly notwithstanding their unrealistic and visionary character. Their crucial role lies in their capacity to help us to make the world a better place. There is no conflict between the demands of (valid) practice and the cultivation of (appropriate) ideals. The bearing of the practical and the ideal stand in mutually supportive cooperation.

Such a perspective of course begs the question against the empiricist and skeptic. He wants to play safe—to have assurances that operations on that empyrean level cannot get us into intellectual or practical mischief. And we must concede to him that such advance assurances cannot be given. We live in a world without guarantees. All we can say is: "Try it, you'll like it—you'll find with the wisdom of hindsight that you have achieved useful results that justify the risks."

The impracticability of an ideal's realization is thus no insuperable obstacle to its validation. This issue of feasibility or infeasibility is simply beside the point, because what counts with an ideal is not the question of its attainment but the question of the overall benefits that accrue from its pursuit. Having and pursuing an ideal, regardless of its impracticability, can yield benefits such as a better life for ourselves and a better world for our posterity. The validation of an ideal thus lies in the pragmatic value of its pursuit. As Max Weber observed with characteristic perspicuity, even in the domain of politics, which has been called "the art of the possible," "the possible has frequently been attained only through striving for something impossible that lies beyond one's reach."[2]

Conflicting Ideals

There are, of course, competing ideals. Aldous Huxley writes:

About the ideal goal of human effort there exists in our civilization and, for nearly thirty centuries, there has existed a very general agreement. From Isaiah to Karl Marx the prophets have spoken with one voice. In the Golden Age to which they look forward there will be liberty, peace, justice, and brotherly love. "Nation shall no more lift sword against nation"; "the free development of each will lead to the free development

[2] "Nicht minder richtig aber ist, dass das Mögliche sehr oft nur dadurch erreicht wurde, dass man nach dem jenseits seiner Kraft liegenden Unmöglichen griff." "Der Sinn der 'Wertfreiheit' in den soziologischen und ökonomischen Wissenschaften" (1917–18), reprinted in *Gesammelte Aufsätze zur Wissenschaftslehre* (Tübingen, 1922), p. 476.

of all"; "the world shall be full of the knowledge of the Lord, as the waters cover the sea."[3]

Susan Stebbing takes Huxley sharply to task here:

In this judgment Mr. Huxley appears to me to be mistaken. There is not now, and there was not in 1937 when Mr. Huxley made this statement, "general agreement" with regard to "the ideal goal of human effort," even in Western Europe, not to mention Eastern Asia. The Fascist ideal has been conceived in sharpest opposition to the values which Mr. Huxley believes to be so generally acceptable, and which may be said to be characteristic of the democratic ideal. The opposition is an opposition with regard to modes of social organization; it . . . necessitates fundamental differences in the methods employed to achieve aims that are totally opposed. The ideal of Fascism is power and the glorification of the State; the ideal of democracy is the development of free and happy human beings; consequently, their most fundamental difference lies in their different conception of the worth of human beings as individuals worthy of respect.[4]

And Stebbing is quite right. Conflicting ideals are a fact of life. Different priorities can be assigned to different values, and to prize A over B is incompatible with prizing B over A. But of course the prospect of goal alternatives no more invalidates one's ideals than the prospect of spouse alternatives invalidates one's marriage. The justification and power of an ideal inhere in its capacity to energize and motivate human effort toward productive results—in short, in its practical efficacy. Ideals may involve unrealism, but this nowise annihilates their impetus or value precisely because of the practical consequences that ensue on our adoption of them.

But what are we to make of the fact that competing and conflicting ideals are possible—that not only can different people have different ideals, but one person can hold several ideals that unkind fate can force into situations of conflict and competition ("the devoted spouse" and "the successful politician," for example)?

Clearly, we have to make a good deal of this. Many things follow, including at least these points: that life is complex and difficult; that perfection is not realizable; that lost causes may claim

---

[3] "Inquiry into the Nature of Ideals and the Methods Employed for Their Realization," in Huxley, *Ends and Means* (London, 1937), p. 1.
[4] *Ideals and Allusions* (London, 1948), pp. 132–33.

our allegiance and conflicts of commitment arise; that realism calls on us to harmonize our ideals even as it requires us to harmonize our other obligations in working and our overall economy of values. It follows, in sum, that we must make various reciprocal adjustments and compromises. But one thing that does not follow is that ideals are somehow illegitimate and inappropriate.

To attain the limits of the possibilities inherent in our powers and potentialities, we must aim beyond them. And just here lies the great importance of the ideal realm. To achieve much we must want more. Human action cannot in general be properly understood or adequately managed without a just appreciation of the guiding ideals that lie in the background. For man's intervention in the real world sometimes is—and often should be— conditioned by his views of the ideal order in whose direction he finds it appropriate to steer the course of events.

This situation has its paradoxical aspect. Ideals may seem to be otherworldly or remote from our practical concerns. But in a wider perspective, they are eminently practical, so that their legitimation is ultimately pragmatic. The imperative to ideals has that most practical of all justifications, namely, that it facilitates the prospects of a more satisfying life. Paradoxical though it may seem, this pragmatic line is the most natural and sensible approach to the validation of ideals.

The general principle of having ideals can be defended along the following lines:

Q: Why should people have ideals at all?

A: Because this is something that is efficient and effective in implementing their pursuit of values.

Q: But why should they care for the pursuit of values?

A: That is simply a part of being human, and thus subject to the fundamental imperative of realizing one's potential of flourishing as the kind of creature one is.

The validity of having ideals inheres in our condition as creatures that dwell in a world of both facts and values.

Admittedly, ideals cannot be brought to actualization as such. Their very "idealized" nature prevents the arrangements they envision from constituting part of the actual furnishings of the world. But in the sphere of human endeavor, we cannot properly explain and understand the reality about us without reference to motivating ideals. The contemplation of what should ideally be is inevitably bound to play an important role in the rational guidance of our actions.

The validation and legitimation of ideals accordingly lie not in their (infeasible) *applicability* but in their *utility* for directing our efforts—their productive power in providing direction and structure to our evaluative thought and pragmatic action. It is in this, their power to move the minds that move mountains, that the validation and legitimation of appropriate ideals must ultimately reside.

The "Unrealism" of Ideals

Ideals are visionary, unrealistic, and utopian. But by viewing the world in the light of their powerful illumination, we see it all the more vividly—and critically. We understand the true nature of the real better by considering it in the light reflected from ideals, and we use this light to find our way about more satisfactorily in the real world. The power of ideals lies in the circumstance that the efficacy of our praxis can be enlarged and enhanced by looking beyond the limits of the practicable. Ideals can render us important service when we "bring them down to earth."

To be sure, our ideals ask too much of us. We cannot attain perfection in the life of this world—not in the moral life, or in the life of inquiry, or in the religious life. Authentic faith, comprehensive knowledge, genuine morality are all idealizations, destinations that we cannot actually reach. They are hyperboles that beckon us ever onward, whose value lies in their practical utility as a motivating impetus in positive directions.

On this account, ideals, despite their superior and splendid appearance, are actually of a subordinate status in point of justification. They are not ultimate ends but instrumental means, subservient to the ulterior values whose realization they facilitate. They are indeed important and valuable, but their worth and validity ultimately reside not in their intrinsic desirability ("wouldn't it be nice if . . .") but in their eminent utility—in their capacity to guide and facilitate the cultivation of the values that they embody.

Such an approach to the issue of legitimating ideals has a curious aspect in its invocation of practical utility for the validation of our ideals. It maintains that the rational appropriateness of our commitment to an ideal lies in its practical utility for our dealings with the real through its capacity to encourage and facilitate our productive efforts. Such an approach does not adopt a "Platonic" view of ideals, in which they are seen as valuable strictly in their own right. Rather, their value is seen as instrumental or pragmatic: ideals are of value not for their own sake but for ours, because of the good effects to be achieved by using them as a compass for steering our thought and action through the shoals and narrows of a difficult world, providing guidelines for acting so as to make one's corner of the world a more satisfying habitat for all.

The Grandeur of Ideals

To say that the ultimate legitimation of ideals is pragmatic is not to say that they are *merely* practical—that they are somehow crass, mundane, and bereft of nobility. By no means! The mode of *justification* of ideals has effectively no bearing on their *nature* at all. Their validation may be utilitarian, but their inherent character can be transcendent. And so there need be nothing crass or mundane about our ideals as such.

With societies and nations, as with individuals, a balanced vision of the good calls for a proportionate recognition of *the domestic impetus* concerned with the well-being of people, home and hearth, stomach and pocketbook, good fellowship, rewarding work, etc. But it also calls for a recognition of *the heroic impetus* concerned with acknowledging ideals, making creative achievements, playing a significant role on the world historical stage, and doing those splendid things on which posterity looks with admiration. Above all, this latter impetus involves the winning of battles not of the battlefield but of the human mind and spirit. The absence of ideals is bound to impoverish a person or a society. Toward people or nations that have the constitutents of material welfare, we may well feel envy, but our *admiration* and *respect* could never be won on this ground alone. Excellence must come into it. And in this excellence-connected domain we leave issues of utility behind and enter another sphere—that of human ideals relating to higher and nobler aspirations.

Homo sapiens is a rational animal. The fact that we are animals squarely places us within the order of nature. But the fact that we are rational exempts us from an absolute rule by external forces. It means that our nature is not wholly *given*, that we are able to contribute in at least some degree toward making ourselves into the sort of creatures we are. A rational creature is inevitably one that has some capacity to let its idealized vision of what it should be determine what it actually is. It is in this sense that an involvement with ideals is an essential aspect of the human condition.

Ideals and Rationality

The fictional nature of ideals accordingly does not destroy their usefulness. To be sure, we do not—should not—expect to bring our ideals to actual realization. Yet an ideal is like the Holy Grail of medieval romance: it impels us onward in the journey and gives meaning and direction to our efforts. Rewards of dignity and worth lie in these efforts themselves, irrespective of the question of actual attainment. When appraising people's lives, the question "What did they endeavor?" is as relevant as the question "What did they achieve?"

The objects at issue in our ideals are not parts of the world's furniture. Like utopias and mythic heroes (or the real-world heroes we redesign in their image by remaking these people into something that never was), ideals are "larger than life." The states of affairs at issue with ideals do not and cannot exist as such. Look about us where we will, we shall not find them actualized. The directive impetus that they give us generally goes under the name of "inspiration." They call to us to bend our efforts toward certain unattainable goals. Yet, though fictions, they are eminently *practical* fictions. They find their utility not in application to the things of this world but in their bearing on the thoughts that govern our actions within it. They are not *things* as such but *thought instrumentalities* that orient and direct our praxis in the direction of realizing a greater good.

Yet ideals, though instruments of thought, are not mere myths. For there is nothing false or fictional about ideals as such—only about the idea of their embodiment in concrete reality. Their pursuit is something that can be perfectly real—and eminently productive. (And it is at this pragmatic level that the legitimation of an ideal must ultimately be sought.)

Still, given the inherent unrealizability of what is at issue, are ideals not indelibly irrational? Here, as elsewhere, we must reckon with the standard gap between aspiration and attainment. In the practical sphere—for example, in craftsmanship or the cultivation of our health—we may *strive* for perfection, but we cannot ever claim to *attain* it. Moreover, the situation in inquiry is exactly parallel, as is that in morality or in statesmanship. The cognitive ideal of perfected science stands on the same level as the moral ideal of a perfect agent or the political ideal of a perfect state. The value of such unrealizable ideals lies not in the (unavailable) benefits of attainment but in the benefits that accrue from pursuit. The view that it is rational to pursue an aim only if we are in a position to achieve its attainment or approximation is simply mistaken. As we have seen, an unattainable end can be perfectly valid (and entirely rational) if the indirect benefits of its pursuit are sufficient—if in striving after it, we realize relevant advantages to a substantial degree. An unattainable ideal can be enormously productive.

The issue of justifying the adoption of unattainable ideals thus brings us back to the starting point of these deliberations— the defense of the appropriateness of fighting for lost causes. Optimal results are often attainable only by trying for too much— by reaching beyond the limits of the possible. The person whose wagon is not hitched to some star or other is not a full-formed human being, is less than he or she can and should be.

It seems particularly incongruous to condemn the pursuit of ideals as contrary to *rationality*. For one thing, rationality is a matter of the intelligent pursuit of appropriate ends, and ideals form part of the framework with reference to which our determinations of appropriateness proceed. No less relevant, however, is the fact that a good case can be made for holding that complete rationality is itself something unrealizable, given the enormously comprehensive nature of what is demanded (for example, by recourse to the principle of total evidence for rationally constituted belief and action). Neither in matters of thought nor in matters of action can we humans ever succeed in being totally and completely rational; we have to recognize that perfect rationality is itself an unattainable ideal. And we must be realistic about the extent to which we can implement this ideal amid the harsh realities of a difficult world. Yet even though total rationality is unattainable, its pursuit is nevertheless perfectly rational because of the great benefits that it palpably engenders. It is thus ironic that the thoroughgoing rationality in whose name the adoption of unattainable ends is sometimes condemned itself represents an unattainable ideal whose pursuit is rationally defensible only by pragmatically oriented arguments of the general sort considered here.

To be sure, this practical sort of validation of ideals leaves untouched the issue of *which* particular values are to prevail. The approach is a general one and thus does not address the justification of particular ideals. It indicates the importance of having some ideals or other, leaving the issue of specific commitments aside. For addressing *this* issue requires more than an abstract analysis of the nature and function of ideals; it calls for articulating and defending a concrete philosophy of life.

But the fact remains that it is important—and crucially so— for a person to have guiding ideals. A life without ideals need not be a life without purpose, but it will be a life without purposes of a sort in which one can appropriately take reflective satisfaction. People for whom values matter so little that they have no ideals are condemned to wander through life disoriented, without guiding beacons to furnish the sense of direction that gives meaning and point to the whole enterprise. Someone who lacks ideals suffers an impoverishment of spirit for which no other resources can adequately compensate.[5]

[5]Some of the lines of thought in this chapter are developed more fully in my *Ethical Idealism* (Berkeley, Calif., 1987).

FOURTEEN

The Meaning of Life

IN THE opening passage of an essay on the meaning of life, the contemporary English philosopher David Wiggins assigns the issue of life's meaning to "the class of questions not in good order, or best not answered just as they stand."[1] But however awkward philosophers may find it to grapple with questions pressed by ordinary people, they cannot in good conscience avoid them.

To be sure, a philosopher must unravel complications. For the question of the meaning of life has a misleading air of directness about it. The closer one looks at it, the more complicated and many-sided it becomes. Specifically, it straightaway admits of four distinctly different interpretations in line with the variant determinations of the schema, "Does (humanity at large/an individual life) have a (purpose/value)?" Its inherent fissures have the consequence that different people approach the issue of life's "meaning" very differently.

Various writers approach the issue from the angle of the question, "Does (the existence of) humanity at large have a *purpose?*" And at this point some theorists see the question as resolved through the distinction between life-inherent and life-transcendent purposes. As Thomas Nagel insists, "Claims of [purposive] justification come to an end within life [itself]. No further justification is needed to take aspirin for a headache, [or]

---

[1] "Truth, Invention, and the Meaning of Life" (1976), reprinted as Essay 3 in his collection *Needs, Values, Truth* (Oxford, 1987).

attend an exhibition of the work of a painter one admires. . . .
No larger context of further purpose is needed to prevent these
acts from being fruitless."[2] This being so with transactions within
life, it is all the more true as regards living one's life as a whole.
Living is itself the purpose of life. In this way, the question of
the meaningfulness of life is often viewed in essentially purposive terms, and is then dismissed with the observation that
living the good life is simply a purpose unto itself, so that no
further venture into ulterior purposiveness is required.

Again, other theorists, proceeding via the idea that a purpose
must be *somebody's* purpose, consider the issue in a theological
light: should we conceive of the existence of mankind as serving
some sort of purposive intention on the part of a creator-God? In
this vein, Kurt Baier treats the issue in such a way that "Is life
meaningful?" is construed as amounting to "Is there room for a
personal relationship between human beings and a supernatural
perfect being ruling and guiding men?"[3] But this approach of
course begs a very large question. Why should it be a relationship with *God* that is needed to make life meaningful?[4] Why
should a relationship to "the world at large" or "other people"
or perhaps even simply to our own selves not be sufficient?

In any event, however, it should be clear that, in deliberat-
ing about the meaning of life, one must be careful to distinguish the question, "Does life have *value*?," from the question,
"Does life have a *purpose*?" When the former question is before
us, the latter need not be brought up at all. One can—quite
appropriately—prize a sunset, or an experience, or a baby as
being something good, something of value, without raising the
instrumental issue of purposes, of what beyond and outside of

[2] *Mortal Questions* (Cambridge, Mass., 1979), p. 12.

[3] *The Meaning of Life* (Canberra, 1957), inaugural lecture.

[4] In Dostoevsky's novel *The Possessed*, Kirlov commits suicide because he
thinks that when we no longer have faith in the existence of God, our life loses
all point and should be ended. But while this thinking is all right, it is clearly
quite foolish thinking. Again, in his article "Truth, Invention, and the Meaning
of Life," Wiggins regards Mozart's rather elitish claim that "we live in this world
to compel ourselves industriously to enlighten one another . . . and to apply
ourselves always to carrying forward the sciences and the arts" as being based
on "the now (I think) almost unattainable conviction that there exists a God
whose purpose ordains certain specific duties for all men." Seeing that Mozart
does not say one word about God here, it is surely problematic to say that a claim
that *might* have a basis in him *must* have this basis.

itself it is good for. And this holds true for life as well. Life can and should be meaningful for its bearer without serving a purpose of some sort.

The issue that is on the minds of ordinary people when they wonder about the meaning of life seems generally to be best represented by a different question: *Does human life have a value?*[5] And a widely held point of view—particularly popular among philosophers of a naturalist orientation—accordingly focuses on the insignificance of people. "The life of a man," David Hume writes, "is of no greater importance to the universe than that of an oyster."[6] Bertrand Russell suggests that, *amour propre* apart, there is no good reason for seeing ourselves as superior to the amoeba. And clearly there is some justice to such a perspective. In nature's vast cosmic scheme of things, we humans are to all appearances cast in the role of an insignificant member of an insignificant species. On the astronomical scale, we are no more than obscure inhabitants of an obscure planet. Nothing we are or do in our tiny sphere of action within the universe's vast reaches of space and time makes any substantial difference in the long run. The glories that were Greece and the grandeur that was Rome have pretty much melted away with the snows of yesteryear. Perhaps the proverb exaggerates in claiming that "it will all be the same 100 years hence." But eventually, the last trace of our feeble human efforts will certainly vanish under the all-consuming ravages of time.

There is in fact much justification for letting a sense of futility and worthlessness pervade our thinking about our own personal place in the universe. It is not implausible to say that we just do not count—that nothing we do really matters in the grand scheme of things. Space is frighteningly large, time awesomely long, causality the interplay of impersonal forces. The universe as modern science portrays it is not a very friendly place. Even here on earth, nature is red in tooth and claw all about us. And people themselves are all too often a frightening

[5] Among recent writers, Robert Nozick sees this point most clearly. He writes: "Meaning involves transcending limits so as to connect with something valuable; meaning is a transcending of the limits of your own value, a transcending of your own limited value. Meaning is a connection with an external value." *Philosophical Explanations* (Cambridge, Mass., 1981), p. 610.

[6] "Of suicide," in E. F. Miller, ed., *Essays Moral, Political, and Literary* (Indianapolis, 1985). One wonders how the universe informed Hume of this.

mixture of phobias and neuroses, with *Homo sapiens* as his own worst enemy, ever ready to destroy the good things that somehow manage to emerge.

Still, this is hardly the end of the matter.

Making a Difference

The issue that people generally have in mind in posing the question of the meaning of life emerges in this light as an *evaluative* question. *Given* the imperfection of human beings and the impermanence of their achievements, and *given* our insignificance in the larger cosmic scheme of things, just exactly what is the *point* of our existence? *Does it really make any difference what we do with our lives?* That, in general terms, is the core question.

Does what we do really matter? But matter to whom? A spectrum of ever-widening possibilities opens up here: ourselves, our near and dear ones, our environing group (co-workers, countrymen), our nation or civilization, our species, intelligent beings in general (those on other planets potentially included), the ideal observer, reality at large (the universe), the world spirit (God). Right from the start, one must resist the temptation to think that what we do only *really* matters if it matters down at the bottom end of this series. One must reject the terrible and profound delusion that making a *real* difference requires making a *big* difference. Size and scale are surely not the only appropriate measures of significance. When something matters even only locally—merely for ourselves—that endows it with a perfectly appropriate value and importance of its own. What is central to the issue of the meaning of life is whether what we do can and does really matter—not necessarily to God or to the universe but to ourselves. It is clearly just this—namely, mattering for us—that counts *for us*, since that is who we are.

The crucial point for meaningfulness, then, is not making a *big* difference, but making a *real* difference. And here, what matters is setting high standards for oneself and effecting one's evaluations in terms of the impersonal criteria that visibly implement those standards. For then the worth of what we do within our sphere of agency and action is something that—however "parochial"—is there objectively for all to see. The reason for looking to objective standards to indicate the meaningfulness of life is not to obtain the approval of others—and not even that of God—but to ensure that approval (valuing) by *anybody*, oneself included, is appropriate. And the standard by which we must surely judge the value of life is not somebody's subjectively grounded personal opinions, but the objective question of whether living offers a prospect for realizing good things.[7] A life that is satisfying for oneself and constructive vis-à-vis others is of value by virtue of these very facts. And this circumstance, which doubtless *does* matter to its bearer, *should* also matter to the rest of us who stand by as observers. It has a meaning that is there for anyone to read.

In an interesting essay on the meaning of life, Robert Nozick proposes to construe the *meaning* of an individual's life in connection with "the wider value context beyond its limits" and its intrinsic value "as centered on, as organized around" the person himself. On this basis, he wonders if the two cannot get out of alignment: "Might there be a conflict between the meaning and the value of a person's life, so that he is forced to consider and to make tradeoffs between these? . . . We care both about the value and the meaning of our life." But Nozick then responds to his own worry by moving on to suggest that "we view these as partial aspects of one [single] underlying thing we care about, let us call it worth."[8] And this is surely correct. Clearly a life's value *for its bearer* and its value *in its wider context* are simply components of *its value at large* (Nozick's "worth"), and it is exactly this that is at issue in assessing the overall meaningfulness of a life.

Man as a Machine?

But does this sort of appreciation really suffice to render life meaningful? Is the value of human life not decisively undermined by the unfolding progress of science—by the ongoing process of discovering that *Homo sapiens* is merely a machine—a mere part of the mechanisms of nature?

In 1748, Julien Offray de la Mettrie published in Leiden his startling treatise *L'Homme machine*, giving vivid expression to the

[7]What sort of good things? There are clearly many of them: happiness, creativity, morality, and so on.

[8]Nozick, *Philosophical Explanations*, pp. 571–627.

naturalism that was part and parcel of the exaggerated dedication to "reason" that typified the intellectual ethics of the era of
the French Revolution. However foolish de la Mettrie's view
may have looked at a time when the most complicated machines
were clockwords and windmills, it certainly seems far less so in
the era of electronic "thinking machines" programmed to dis-
play "artificial intelligence." Perhaps man is, after all, no more
than a machine?

The shock effect of the idea of man's being a machine lies in
the very fallacious impression that this circumstance would
somehow *change* what man in fact is. For we incline to think that
this would mean that man would thereby be devalued, that human life would then cease to be significant. But how does this
follow? If one accepts that our bodies consist of chemical elements—mainly water—whose market value is but a few dollars,
does that have any implications for our value as *persons*? Why
should it? The closer one looks, the less apparent the reason.

But if man were a machine, would that not mean that he has
no soul? Well . . . would it? What is "a soul" anyway? Clearly it
is not some sort of physical component of one's body—like a
kidney or a liver. Presumably a human soul is what it does—its
being resides in a person's capacity to think, feel, aspire, love,
and the like. Even if man were a machine, that would not mean
that people lack souls. On the contrary—the consequence would
simply be that machines can have souls. If the being of a soul lies
in what a besouled creature can do, then if machines can do
what people can, they too will have souls. If man indeed were a
machine, the net effect would be not to dehumanize man, but to
produce a drastic change in our understanding of the nature of
machines by totally humanizing (at least) some of them.

People sometimes feel themselves threatened by the
argument:

1. *Man is a machine.*
2. *Machines cannot do X (cannot have feelings, have free will, etc.).*

Therefore: *Man does not do X (cannot have feelings, have free
will, etc.).*

But to maintain (2) is in effect to beg the question if (1) is as-
serted. All we can say is that *typical* machines do not behave in
this way. But a human being, if indeed a machine, is certainly
not a typical machine. The shock value of claiming that people

are machines comes from the circumstance that it is all too easy to make the fallacious leap from the contention "Man is a machine" to the conclusion "Man is a *typical* machine." But of course this no more follows than from "Man is an animal" there follows the far-fetched conclusion "Man is a *typical* animal."

Dictionaries generally define "machine" in such terms as a mechanical or electronically operated device designed for performing a predesignated task. Given *this* sort of specification, men and animals are obviously not machines. But this finding is not particularly interesting for the discussion because it rules out from the very start any prospect of considering the idea that one might be a machine. Such verbal force majeure apart, the question remains: is man a machine—albeit an organic, biological rather than mechanical, artifactual one?

To pursue this question intelligently would in the first instance require providing a pretty exact specification of just exactly what a machine is. And this is certainly not easy to come by. The breathtaking modern development in the capacities and complexities of "thinking machines" that makes it possible to contemplate man's being a machine without ludicrous incongruity have also cost us any secure intellectual grasp on just what it is to be a machine. Nobody has yet provided a clear and cogent explanation of just what "a machine" is in the current scheme of things. And in the absence of such an explanation, the question "Is man a machine?" poses an imponderable issue.

But if it were to turn out in the end to be appropriate to categorize man as a machine, this eventuation would flatly fail to dehumanize us. If man is indeed a machine, then he is certainly a very peculiar one—one that is organic, intelligent, capable of feeling, suffering, loving, etc. If man is a machine, then machines can do some pretty nonmachine–sounding things. The result would be to revolutionize not just our ordinary idea of *man* but our ordinary idea of *machine* as well.

Sometimes theorists try to bend the issue into other shapes. For example, might human beings be made artificially—somehow synthesized in a laboratory? But of course even if this could be done, it would not show we are machines. It would simply go to show that the range of things one can make in a laboratory includes not only chemicals and machines but also (perhaps more surprisingly) people.

To summarize. There is no good reason to think that we humans are indeed simply machines. But even if we were, we would be machines of an unusual sort—things that are, in principle, by no means theoretically impossible, namely, machines endowed with free will, machines not designed and programmed by other agents but actually evolved in a way that puts them in charge of what they do themselves. Man's being a machine would not downgrade the value of human life, but could leave unaffected the value and stature of some (pretty nonstandard) machines.

Free Will

But are we indeed in charge of our actions? For what of the dread prospect that we are mere automata in that our will is not free, and all our actions merely the result of the play of natural forces beyond our control?

People who deny free will generally proceed on the basis of contemplating a physical order of natural process that determines all the world's events, human actions included, through the operation of impersonal causes. On this basis, they launch on the following plausible argumentation:

1. *Whatever people do falls within the scope of laws of nature.*

2. *Actions falling within the scope of laws of nature are for this very reason necessitated in nature's impersonal order and are accordingly not free.*

Therefore: *Everything people do is determined by a causal necessitation operating independently of the wishes and choices of human agents.*

On this telling, our actions are every bit as much necessitated by the impersonal forces of nature as is the downhill flow of water or the motion of a billiard ball. They only *seem* governed by our choices and decisions—in fact, they are the product of an impersonal necessity that works in and through our bodies.

This familiar line of reasoning is seriously flawed, however. To have free will is in the first instance to be in a position to act from motives, goals, and values that one has—to have one's actions proceed from the "motivational" sectors of one's thinking via one's own decisions and choices. It is a matter of the "inner," thought-embedded determination of what one does, and not a matter of the severance of one's actions from any and all determinations whatsoever. A free act is one that is not free of *all* determination, but one that is free of determination *of a certain particular sort*, namely, from determiners that operate in detachment from one's own wants, preferences, wishes, and the like. Its agent "could have done otherwise," all right, but only if the agent's choices and decisions had been different—which itself could have happened only if the agent's values, goals, and decisions had been different. No adequate explanation in the order of causal determination can factor the agent out of it. (2) is accordingly false.

But is our capacity to implement our own agenda—to act on the basis of our own feelings, wishes, desires, preferences, etc.— really enough to render us free agents? For what if our agenda is itself set by factors beyond our control? Then everything hinges on the *nature* of that "external" determination—on the sort of mechanism at issue. In particular, if this is a matter of manipulation by an external controller, thereby rendering our own putative decisions subject to the will of another, then the matter stands very ill for freedom.

Freedom of action is a matter of being in control of one's doings. It is a matter of autonomy, of independence of other *wills*— of hinging on one's own choices, preferences, wishes, etc., and being able to function independently of the choices, wishes, etc., of other agents. Freedom pivots on an agent's independence of other *agents* and their machinations—not of an independence of operative *causes*. After all, all of us—free agents included—are part of the world's fabric of lawful operation, and everything we do is to this extent conditioned and conceivably even "determined" by factors of nature and nurture over which we have no control. But *this* sort of "impersonal determination" has nothing to do with freedom of the will. For what is crucial here is simply the matter of a determination *by other wills*. What freedom precludes is a causality that bypasses the will of the agent—either because it involves no wills at all (i.e., no decisions, preferences, choices, etc.) or because it involves only the wills of *other* agents.

We thus arrive at the doctrine of *compatibilism*—the argument that freedom of the will is compatible with a softened determinism in the order of natural processes because "freedom" is not a matter of exemption from causal determinism but itself involves a determination of sorts, namely, one in which those "events" that are represented by decisions, choices, etc., and those "dispositions" that are involved in wishes, preferences, etc., are crucial for the adequate explanation of human actions. Freedom and determinism are simply not mutually exclusive contraries. In principle, an action can be at once determined *and* free, as long as the pattern of determination maintains its linkage to the wishes and choices of the agent.

Science as the Destroyer of Values?

All the same, if the world is more or less as physical science nowadays depicts it, does this not deprive life of meaning and value? Does science not abolish any room for value in the world's scheme of things?

But how could it possibly do so? Physical science tells us a *causal* story; it describes the mechanics of how things work in the world. It does not undermine the value of life because it does not address questions of value at all. The sound of a violin may be no more than the play of air waves caused by the vibration of dried cat's-guts. But what has that got to do with the beauty or cacophony of the music? What matters for value is not the causal dimension of process, but the experiential dimension of product as it bears on the course of our lives. The issue of the meaningfulness of life is a value question. And this is something that science does not affect in any negative way. Science is not and cannot be at odds with value because the questions of valuation are ones that it does not address at all.

In the final analysis, science has to leave the world as it finds it—its mission is to examine and explain the real, not to destroy it. In explaining how it is that people go about valuing things, science does not show that value is somehow unreal—any more than in explaining color vision, science shows that color is somehow unreal. Value attributions, like color attributions, are rooted in experience. And while science can presumably *explain* experience, it does not and indeed cannot show that it is somehow unreal or insignificant.

It is the characterizing mission of natural science to enable us to explain the world's processes and eventuations, and to do this in such a way that we can test the adequacy of our explanations by means of effective technological intervention. But explanation and understanding are one thing and experiencing another. (We can *explain* how bats fly blind but cannot *experience* it.) And values arise in the experiential sector. To explain how people have them is one thing, actually to possess them another.

The test of value is the test of experience—conducting a life that proceeds on its basis. Evaluation, like inquiry, is a matter of inference from the data of experience. In *this* regard, both are alike. But we deal with information on the one hand, and with appreciation on the other. Different *dimensions* of experience are at issue. And it is this difference of thematic dimension that averts any prospect of a clash. There is no reason of principle why we cannot validate value judgments in a world constituted as the science of the day maintains—and this includes judgments about the value of life itself.

Activism

But just how does experience bear on the vindication of values? One can, in theory, see the index of inductive soundness to lie in:

What pleases me?
What suits my purposes (ends, goals)?
What I can appropriately deem for the best with reference to
   —my own interests?
   —the interests of others?
   —the good of "the larger scheme of things"?

The evaluative aspect of life's meaningfulness obviously requires us to move well down this list. The standard for proper valuation in this context is clearly something larger than oneself, one's wishes, one's interests. What makes one's life meaningful is not simply a matter of one's own personal benefits, wishes, or interests. More is involved than any merely subjective frame of reference. That "larger scheme of things" does indeed come into it.

The crux for meaningfulness is that life affords us the opportunity of making a difference—a positive contribution to the totality of realized value. What ultimately renders life meaningful is not the "pursuit of happiness" but the "pursuit of excellence." A life is rendered meaningful through the promotion of values—the fostering of the good on however small a scale. Nothing grand need be at issue. Or, rather, even mundane things can in this context achieve the level of grandeur: being a good friend or a good neighbor or a good companion, for example. It becomes something positive through the furtherance, to the best of one's efforts—however ineffectual—of the values that people appropriately hold dear.

Cosmic history is a process of development. Chemical elements and their properties were not present in the first microseconds after the big bang. Astronomical objects (stars, planets, and the like) took much longer to develop. And life took longer still. Intelligent beings, with their goals, purposes, and values, came even later. These sorts of things (values, purposes, goals) are doubtless later comers. But the fact remains that with the emergence of intelligent agents they are indeed there—not as *given* but as *developed*. And with their emergence, purposeful action and rational evaluation came to be possible in a heretofore purposeless and value-free cosmos. Intelligent life can and does have a meaning because value emerges with the emergence of intelligence.

Kant stood in awe before internal and external nature ("the moral law within; the starry heavens above"). Hegel stood in awe before social reality and the historical processes of its formation (the "Spirit"). A true humanist, by contrast, will stand in awe before man—but not so much man as he actually (and most imperfectly) is, but man as he can get himself to be if he puts his mind to it.

Some modicum of yearning for something "larger than life"— for transcendent goods and values to endow one's life with a value beyond itself—is an essential aspect of the makeup of an intelligent agent. Miguel de Unamuno was wrong.[9] The ultimate evil for us is not our mortality—the inescapable prospect of the termination of our personal *self*. It is not death we fear as much as meaninglessness and pointlessness: death is merely the ending of our life. Bad though this may be, there looms the threat of something far worse. The annihilation of everything we value and prize and stand for is the ultimate evil. It is not so much

[9] See his 1913 classic *Del sentimiento trágico de la vida*, ed. P. Felix Garcia (Madrid, 1982).

personal survival that we yearn for as vindication or validation—the sense that our efforts need not be wholly in vain, and
all our endeavors in life an exercise in futility. Precisely because
true "self-actualization" is a matter of striving for the best, what
ultimately counts for us is not so much the survival of our *selves*
as the survival of our *values*.

Every person who is not totally incapacitated, who has some
capacity for agency at all, has the possibility of acting for the
good—of doing the better instead of the worse. Every such life
therefore is potentially of value as an agent for enlarging the
world's stock of good. Human life *is* of value because it affords
us the chance to promote value within the world's scheme of
things.

Defeat does not come to the life of an individual through
death. For things being as they are, death is inevitable and itself
forms an integral part of human life. Nor does defeat come
through a failure to achieve success—for this, in large measure,
is something fortuitous, something outside the range of our control. Defeat and failure in life are always self-inflicted—the willful persistence in that most sorry of all human failings, the failure to try to make something of ourselves through the endeavor
to contribute to the world's ever-insufficient stock of the good.
And the price of failure is the stark dilemma between inhuman-
ity on the one side and undergoing a deserved dissatisfaction
with oneself on the other—the realization of some deeper level
of thought that one has failed as a human being, that one has
conducted one's life in a way that the rational side of one's being
will not allow oneself to approve of. For we suffer a small defeat
in life with each failure to harmonize action and evaluation—
each time we do something we cannot in our heart of hearts approve of. And a life in which such small defeats become massive,
prevailing, and predominant is a life whose bearer has condemned himself to utter failure.

And at this point there is no reason for being intimidated by a
sense of impotence. For the crucial issue here is that what sort of
people we strive to make of ourselves—a matter in which endeavor counts every bit as much as accomplishment and which
lies wholly in our own control. The crux resides in this matter of
striving to make the best of ourselves—of self-optimization.

Value is self-engendering. Our lives become the bearers of value through the very fact of their affording us an opportunity to endeavor to make them valuable.

"Does life have meaning?" is thus not a question of the same sort as "Does Brazil have petroleum deposits?" We are not going to resolve it by some sort of observational search. It is going to take theoretical reflection. The issue ultimately comes down to this: "Can we make better sense than we otherwise could of the world and of our lives within it by proceeding on the supposition that human life can be a thing of value?" And interestingly enough, this issue of valuation is a significant measure, a self-fulfilling one. We can *endow* life with meaning and value in the course of proceeding on the supposition that these things belong there. "Is life meaningful?" is a question somewhat like "Are people friendly?" Even as we can often render people friendly by viewing and treating them as friends, so we can often render life meaningful by viewing and treating it as such.

Life can be *made* meaningful by living the sort of life (a sort that includes many instances!) that any sensible person would find meaningful, because it is in living our lives in a certain way that we can make them into things of value.[10] Life can be rendered meaningful—for anyone and in all circumstances—through the cultivation of rationally merited self-respect.

So ultimately the question of the meaning of life is not of the passive form "can we *find* meaning in life?," but of an active one: "Can we *make* a meaningful life?" The real issue is this: can we make ourselves into the kind of people whose lives can plausibly be deemed bearers of value by anyone—ourselves included—who uses standards that reasonably qualify as appropriate?

The "existentialists" are right in this regard, at least, that the question of the meaning of life is ultimately not a matter of *finding* meaning in life, but a matter of *making* life meaningful—of endeavoring to live our lives in such a way that a reasonable person can appropriately see them as meaningful. The question "Does life have meaning?" ultimately comes down to, "Do I have

---

[10] Note, however, that life is not made meaningful by mastering formulas, by learning and subscribing to claims on the order of "The meaning of life is . . . ." It is one thing to recognize that a certain sort of life has value—a "full and productive" life, say, or a life "dedicated to the service of others"—but it is a very different thing to *live* such a life.

the possibility of living the sort of life that is meaningful in my own sight when I take the trouble to view the matter rationally?"

The crux is that life has meaning because the human person is itself an item of value. For value inheres in what people are— a worth that, in turn, is determined by what people can do, namely, understand, act, and aspire. Human life at large has a meaning precisely because individual lives can be of value in affording their bearers an opportunity for the achievement or furtherance of good results. Whether one succeeds or fails in one's efforts, one can at least try to promote the realization of values. And just herein—in the possibility of effort, of aspiration and struggle, achievement and failure—lies the values and thus the meaningfulness of human existence. It is not in human-ity's *achievements* that the value of life resides, but in its irre-pressible determination to exert its *efforts* in the endeavor to avert nothingness.[11]

[11] It is impossible to write sensibly on this subject without sounding preachy. Contemporary philosophers seem to want to have it both ways. Witness David Wiggins, who informs us in the closing passage of his above-cited discussion that the account he advocates would accommodate "the insight that to see a point in living someone has to be such that he can like himself" and shortly thereafter quotes with enthusiasm F. H. Bradley's obiter dictum: "If to show theoretical interest in morality and religion is taken as setting oneself up as a teacher or preacher, I would rather leave these subjects to whoever feels that such a role suits him." Philosophers, like other folk, like to have their cake and eat it too.

FIFTEEN

On Faith and Belief

IT IS POSSIBLE—and plausible—to distinguish between two very different approaches to the issue of a person's stance toward the existence of God. On the one hand, one can ask the following family of questions:

Does X believe or disbelieve in the existence of God?
Just what sort of God is it in which X believes or disbelieves?
On the basis of what sorts of reasons does X believe or disbelieve in God?

The approach reflected in these questions is what will here be characterized as *doxastic*, because of its focus on the issue of belief (Greek *doxa* = belief, opinion). The other approach, which for convenience we will term a value-oriented, *axiological* approach, takes a very different, distinctively evaluative line (Greek *axioō* = to deem worthy, to value). It pivots on the three related, but nevertheless very different questions:

Does X want God to exist—is this something seen as desirable (yearned for or hoped for)?
Just what sort of God is it that X desires (yearns or hopes for)?
For what sorts of reasons is it that X desires (yearns or hopes for) the existence of God?

It is clear that distinctly divergent approaches are involved here: the first set of questions looks to *beliefs*, and the second to *wishes*—to hopes or desires about the sort of God we would want if we could have our way in the matter. The former issue pivots on a person's *convictions*. But the latter pivots on a person's *values*. Very different things are at issue. In principle, one can either believe in the reality of a God whose existence one does not welcome or yearn for the existence of a God in whose reality one does not believe. In a way, axiological atheism is a far more drastic position than doxastic atheism, since axiological atheists, irrespective of whether or not they believe in God, would *prefer* to have him nonexistent and would do away with him if they could.

For the axiological theist, the commitment to God is a matter of value-based desire, and at most hope, rather than a probatively assured confidence derived from the evidential impetus of revelation, or mystical encounter, or rational demonstration. In the backdrop of axiological theism there looms the large and absorbing issue of *what sort of God one would have if one could get one's way*. This question looks toward something that is essentially utopian—a mind's-eye view of an ideal order that one would have if only one could manage it. A fundamentally evaluative position is at issue, rather than one that bears on existence as such, a position that reflects one's deepest hopes, wants, and fears. Does one want a God who would avenge one's wrongs and wreak havoc on one's enemies, a God that labors for the advancement of one's tribe or clan (or assures victory to one's side in battle), a God of justice to punish wrongs and reward good deeds, or a God of love, understanding, and forgiveness? Clearly, a great range of variation exists, and people betray much about themselves when they position themselves in such a spectrum.

Doxastic and Axiological Theism

As regards the doxastic approach, three distinct positions are possible: to believe, to disbelieve, or to suspend judgment (that is, neither believe or disbelieve). The axiological approach likewise accommodates three positions, according as one is positive, negative, or indifferent on the matter of welcoming (wishing for, hoping for) the existence of God.[1] The doxastic approach

---

[1] Specifically, one must distinguish two negative positions here. On the one hand, there is the position of the person X who does not want a being answering

views the issue of God's existence in a straightforwardly *factual* light; the axiological approach views the issue in an *evaluative* light. A belief-oriented approach to God puts prime emphasis on convictions and creeds; there is an aura of scholasticism about its endorsement of existential and descriptive *theses* with respect to the God-conception at issue. An axiological approach to God proceeds on the side of will rather than intellect: its concern is with an evaluative focus on desire, wish, and hope. For all these differences, though, both approaches share one concern in common, namely, the central question of how God is conceived of. And this is as it should be. For this matter of the conceptualization of God is obviously something pivotal for a person's stance toward religion.

Atheism—unlike agnosticism—does not as such relieve its exponent of the burden of articulating a conception of God. Denying the existence of God does not free one from coming to grips with the *conception* of God. Quite aside from the matter of believing or disbelieving in God's existence, there remains the significant, preliminary issue of the descriptive ideas that someone has regarding the God whose existence or nonexistence this person is disposed to endorse. Is it the God who dwells on the pinnacle of the Homeric Mount Olympus? the God of Abraham and Isaac and Jacob? the God of Plato's *Timaeus*? the God of Aristotle's *Metaphysics*? the God of a neo-Aristotelian like Aquinas? There is of course enormous scope for variation here across the spectrum from crudity to refinement. In fact, from the standpoint of a thoughtful believer, there is something to be said for preferring a disbeliever with an enlightened conception of God to a believer who conceives of God crudely, as a partisan Oriental potentate whose prime object is to promote this believer's own personal interests and power and to punish his enemies.

Deliberations about the meaning of life are sometimes beclouded by the idea that the existence of God is a requisite for human life to be meaningful. But this very problematic view ig-

---

to the god-description D to exist (perhaps because this person never even thought of this possibility:
$$\sim WX(E!G_D).$$
On the other hand, there is the position of the person X who wants a being answering to the god-description at issue not to exist:
$$WX(\sim E!G_D).$$
It is clear that the second position is logically stronger than the first.

nores the difference between doxastic and axiologic theism. For the axiological theist, the crucial questions are not (1) does God exist, and (2) if so, does he approve of what I do with my life? Rather, the crucial questions are (1) do I have a conception of God that is worthy of this name, and (2) if this God, as so conceived, did indeed exist, then would he approve of what I do with my life?

This distinction suggests that the *existence* of God is not as such a pivotal issue for the question of the meaningfulness of our lives. Rather, the crux lies in the *hypothetical* question, "Do we conduct our lives in such a way that the sort of God we ourselves deem worth having would, were he to exist, approve of the way we manage the business of life?" Here it is the idea of God that serves to set a high standard. And the question of whether our lives are meaningful is in the final analysis the question of whether the way we conduct ourselves realizes the values to which such a standard calls us.

The conception of God thus emerges as a point of reference for shaping our lives. It can play the role of something of a North Star that we see, not with the eye of the body, but with the eye of the mind, and use to guide our journey in a difficult world. Contemplating the mere idea of God, will, in raising the question of how *he would* evaluate what we do, pose the question of how *we should* carry out this evaluation.

It is, in fact, this aspect of the matter that makes religion so important a topic in philosophical anthropology. Clearly, the *sort* of God one is committed to is going to make an enormous difference for the sort of person one is. Whether people are atheists or believers, their conception of God speaks volumes about their personalities. For that conception generally serves them as a measuring instrument—a standard for assessing the value of human actions and the worth of all those other "things in heaven and on earth" that are encompassed in their philosophy. "By their gods shall ye know them" is by no means an implausible dictum: people's ideas in this regard are immensely illuminating about their stance toward the world and man's place within it. Even dedicated atheists reveal a great deal about themselves in their conception of the sort of God or gods that they propose to reject.

What makes people coreligionists in the setting of an axiological theism is not a commonality of *belief* but a commonality of *desire*. In this context, "the faithful" of a given orientation need not constitute a doxastic community of shared belief, but might instead constitute an axiological community of shared values and hopes. The operative theology is not so much cognitive as attitudinal.

Axiological theism is not to be identified with what is generally known as *fideism*. For what is at issue is not a belief undertaken at the behest of the will rather than the intellect—of willing to believe or trying to believe (as per what Aquinas characterized as "an act of the intellect in which it is moved to assent by the will" (*actum intellectus secundum quod movetur a voluntate ad assentiam*).[2] Something along the lines of a Jamesian "will to believe" is not required by an axiological theism. Its pivot—to reemphasize—is the evaluative matter of desire and hope, not the cognitive matter of belief. Accordingly, an all-out axiological atheism takes a very strong and not particularly sympathetic line. It goes beyond the daunting dictum that "God is dead" to add "And good riddance too." It takes the position of the person who says, "I just can't think of any sort of being worthy of the name of God whose existence I would be prepared to welcome." Such a position does not say much about God, but it speaks volumes about the person at issue.

Problems of Atheism

In principle, even a doxastic atheist can be an axiological theist. That is, even the people who think that God's nonexistence is a sure thing can regret this and wish with all their heart that the matter stood otherwise.

The status of axiological theism would be substantially altered, to be sure, if the evaluative stance at issue were demonstrably futile, with all hope forlorn because one could somehow establish in a knockdown, drag-out way that a God conceived of along a particular line was altogether infeasible. If doxastic atheists could actually *prove* their case outright, then axiological

---

[2] Aquinas, ST ɪɪ, ii, 4, 2c. See also Kant's "moralische Denkungsart der Vernunft im Fürwahrhalten desjenigen, was für die theoretische Erkenntnis unzulänglich ist" (moral operation of reason in adjudging true that which is simply inaccessible to theoretical cognition). *Critique of Judgment*, sec. 91.

theism would be reduced to mere wishful thinking. But outside of pure mathematics such demonstrations of nonexistence are difficult, if not impossible. For a shortage or even absence of evidence for existence does not transmute into a demonstration of nonexistence. And so, the axiological theist can occupy the ecological niche left by an absence of outright atheism. As long as one is agnostic—is prepared to consider as a viable prospect at least the possibility that a Judeo-Christian God (say) might exist—axiological theism is a viable option.

But can axiological theism not be foreclosed and the issue settled straightforwardly in atheism's favor by mere considerations of the burden of proof? Not really. To be sure, on the *ontological* side, the atheist can plausibly saddle his opponent with the burden of proof: "You believe that a God answering to description G exists. This is a positive contention, and it is up to you to prove it—subject to the old legal principle that the burden of proof lies with someone who takes a positive position on an issue (*ei incumbit probatio qui dicit, non qui negat*). In the absence of appropriate evidence or argument for the existential claim at issue, my negative position prevails. As long as you do not dislodge me from it, I carry off victory in the controversy." And so the atheist argues that a debate about the existence of God properly begins from a presumption of atheism, with the onus of proof on the side of the theist. And the atheist takes this position with substantial justice.[3] For with such factual claims the burden of proof is, as usual, on the affirmative side. Clearly, an existential claim must receive the backing of evidential substantiation if it is to qualify as rationally warranted. However, this sort of probative strategy regarding factual contentions is not available to the atheist with respect to the *axiological* approach. "A God of description G is desirable" and "A God of description G is not desirable" (or, more generally, "X has a high value" and "X has a low value") are contentions that lie on the same plane. Positive positions confront us on both sides of an evaluative controversy, and argumentation is called for either way. In the context of axiological theism, the atheist enjoys no probative advantage over his opponent.

[3] For a fuller development of this position, see Anthony Flew, "The Presumption of Atheism," *Canadian Journal of Philosophy*, 2 (1972): 29–46.

Antitheological Psychology

Of course, the well-trodden path of antitheological psychologizing is still open to the opponent of axiological theism. The general line is all too familiar: "You see the traditional monotheistic God as desirable merely because he answers a psychological need of yours. You have a psychological yearning for acceptance, validation, support. Your God is a mere parent-substitute to meet the needs of a weak and dependent creature."

But this sort of facile psychologizing ultimately cuts both ways. For the axiological theist can readily respond along the following lines: "You see the traditional monotheistic God as undesirable because you find the very idea threatening. You atheists too are 'God fearing,' but in a rather different sense. You are *afraid* of God. You have an adolescent's fixated fear of condemnation by authority. Your atheism roots in self-contempt. Recognizing what an imperfect creature you yourself are, you have a fear of being judged and found wanting. The very idea of God is threatening to you because you fear the condemnation of an intelligent observer who knows what you think and do. You are enmeshed in an adolescent aversion to parental disapproval."

And this psychologizing counterargument is not without surface plausibility. Many people are in fact frightened by the prospect of believing in God because they ultimately have a contempt of themselves. They feel *threatened* by the thought that God might exist, because they feel that, were it so, God would not approve of them. For them, atheism is a security shield of sorts that protects them against an ego-damaging disapproval by somebody who "knows all, sees all." Atheists are not infrequently people on whose inmost nature the vice of self-contempt has its strongest hold. Pretensions to the contrary notwithstanding, the atheist's actual posture is generally not a self-confident independence of spirit, but a fear of being judged.

In this regard, then, there is simply a standoff in regard to a Freud-style psychologizing about religion. Those psychologizing arguments that impute rationally questionable motives to the believer are not difficult to revise and deploy as arguments against the atheist. Psychologizing is a sword that cuts both ways in regard to axiological theism. Both sides can easily play the game of projecting, on a speculative basis, a daunting variety of intellectually nonrespectable motives for holding the point of view that they oppose.

Doxastic Versus Axiological Theism

So much, then, for the psychology of the matter. The fact remains that from the angle of probative warrant—of justificatory validation—doxastic and axiological theism stand on very different footings. Doxastic theism involves an existential claim for whose rational warranting some sort of *evidence* is needed—alternatively demonstrative (as per the ontological argument) or experiential (as per a mystical communion) or somehow inductive (as per the cosmological argument) or based on a special cognitive source (such as revelation). One way or another, evidential confirmation is required. Axiological theism is something very different. It involves no existential claim or presupposition. It pivots merely on a desire, a hope, or a wish.

But how can one rationally validate this sort of thing? Can a wish be legitimated and justified? The validation of wishes is no doubt a large and complicated topic. But, clearly, at the core of the matter lies the task of showing that the thing wished for actually *merits* being desired—that it is something valuable and deserving of preference. Hopes and wishes are properly validated in the order of values.

For the rational person desires what he or she deems to be good. Such a person desires what is desirable—is worthy of desire. With such people—who may well be few and far between—the situation is exactly the reverse of what Spinoza maintained regarding ordinary mortals when he wrote: "We do not endeavor, will, seek after, or desire because we judge a thing to be good. On the contrary, we judge a thing to be good because we endeavor, will, seek after, and desire it."[4] Rational people value things precisely because they are convinced that those things are of value.

Perhaps the most effective process for validating a hope or de-

---

[4] "Nihil nos conari, velle, appetere, neque cupere, quia id bonum esse judicamus; sed contra, nos propterea aliquid bonum esse judicare quia id conamus, volumus, appetimus, atque cupimus." *Ethics*, part 3, prop. 9, scholium.

sire involves proceeding in a way that is at once experimental and experiential, namely, by trying and seeing and finding it suitably rewarding—in actuality or perhaps only by way of a thought-experiment. Our desire for something can in principle be legitimated as rational by looking at lives lived under the guiding aegis of this hope or desire and assessing how satisfying they really are to the bearers. In general, one can verify the validity of desires experientially—by trying and seeing that a life based on the pursuit of the desired object is found by those who actually live it to be worthwhile and satisfying. Axiological theism can and should meet the test of experience—essentially through "an experiment in living." The validation of the position can be had by examining and assessing the quality of the lives lived by those who look on God's place in reality's scheme of things with the eye of hope and desire.

Thus while even axiological theists must indeed—if rational—somehow validate the hopes and desires on which their position is predicated, there is no reason of general principle why this requirement cannot be met in a sensible way. The circumstance that the position is fundamentally evaluative certainly does not mean that the element of rationality is absent. For while the value orientation at issue indeed needs justification, it can receive it in principle along the experiential lines just contemplated.

Theological Utopianism

But is axiological theism not just a matter of "wishful thinking"—on the order of investing hope in the existence of Santa Claus or the Easter Bunny? One does not really believe that such "desirable beings" actually exist, after all, but is merely inclined to agree that it would be nice if they did.

However, this skeptical analogy ignores a deep difference regarding the presently pivotal issue of the legitimating *validation* of such hopes. For with the Easter Bunny and its cognates, the underlying value rationale is of questionable propriety. After all, its basis is strictly selfish; if we desire the existence of such beings, it is solely because of the *material benefits* that this would bestow on us or those near and dear—surely a very suspect and problematic justification for a hope or desire in point of fundamental values. With God, however, the situation is, or should be, very different. His realization is to be seen as desirable not because it would render the world more *pleasant,* but because it would render the world more *excellent,* and not because it *benefits* us in selfish advantage, but because it *challenges* us to make the best and most of ourselves. Realization of the hope at issue is desirable not merely because it promotes our material advantage, but because it signalizes the significance of higher, "spiritual" values, commitment to which need not *please* us but will *improve* us in stimulating us to a greater effort for the good, impelling us to make of ourselves the very best that we can be. The crucial difference is that the values at issue are not crass but elevating.

From the angle of legitimation, the two desires accordingly stand on a very different basis. The idea of God as a supreme being that loves, sustains, and cares about us represents a paradigmatic embodiment of significant values: parental solicitude, understanding, loving-kindness. Nothing comparable is at issue with the Easter Bunny. Because it "would be nice if" such a being existed simply and solely because of the pleasant things it supposedly does for people—in particular, children—on Easter morning, what is at issue is strictly merely self-serving material interest. With axiological theism, by contrast, what is at issue is a certain sort of utopian aspiration for ourselves and the conduct of our lives—a willingness to be challenged to make the best and most of our opportunities for the good in this world, an absence of fear in the face of an inspection of hearts, and a preparedness to be held accountable by a deity that, while well disposed to us, nevertheless knows us to the very depths of our being. Here, then, there is a commitment to certain goals and values that—unlike those of material advantage—conduce to our self-development on the basis of our best or real interests. And this circumstance distances the issue from that of the Easter Bunny. The validation of the appropriateness of the hope at issue with axiological theism stands on a very different and far more solid footing.

"Nevertheless"—so a skeptic may urge—"what you are doing here is merely justifying a *desire* for God's existence. And that really does not address my concerns. What I really care about is validating a belief in his existence, and not just legitimating a hope or desire for it. As I see it, hope and wish just aren't enough for *real* religiosity." In religion as in epistemology, skeptics like to ease their task by setting exaggeratedly high standards for their opponents. But so be it! We must consider also how hope and belief are interrelated.

The Interrelationship of Hope and Belief

The question of how doxastic and axiological theism are connected with one another bears two very different aspects—the one logical, the other rather personalistic and, as it were, ethical. Logically the situation is straightforward. There is in fact no inferential transition between axiological and doxastic theism. The sort of God one wants and would welcome is one thing, and one's belief in God's existence is something else again, something very different. From a purely logical point of view, the twain need never meet.

But from a personalistic point of view, the matter stands quite differently. A close, two-way connection obtains. For on the one hand, doxastic theism slides into axiology. If one genuinely *believes* in God—if the being whose existence one accepts is indeed a *God* worthy of the name (rather than some vast demonic power that stridently demands acknowledgment and obeisance)—then it is surely right and proper that the being one believes in be the sort of God that one values, the sort of God whose existence one would deem worthy of approbation. Accordingly, since whatever God one may believe in must—if worthy of the name—be a being one regards as deserving of being desired by sensible people, it seems that an axiological approach should, at any rate, be a needed *appendix* to a doxastic theology.

But what of the reverse situation—the transition from an axiological to a doxastic theism? It is, of course, possible to view one's axiologically geared conception of the sort of God one would welcome as representing something that is simply being "too good to be true" for actual belief. One may perhaps hardly dare to believe in the existence of so desirable a being. But understandable though this may be, it manifests a certain personal shortcoming, a defeatist failure of nerve.

Such a failure is certainly not a failure of intellect, but rather a sort of *moral* failure that has something deeply regrettable about it. The failure to give reality the benefit of the doubt on the matter of its containing a God is akin to the (understandable but unfortunate) attitude of someone whom others have let down and who turns misanthropic, no longer willing to invest hope in other people and unwilling to give them the benefit of the doubt. It is certainly not in point of intellect but rather in point of character that such a person is deficient. For of the many forms of human failing, the failure of imagination is one of the saddest. And one of the gravest failures of imagination is that of the person who cannot manage to project the conception of a God worthy of ardent desire—a God whose nonbeing would be the occasion for genuine grief. Compared with this, an inability to imagine a friend worth having or a spouse worth loving is a pale shadow—though all alike betoken a regrettable impoverishment of personality of the same general sort. Sensible people would clearly prefer to number among their friends someone who was willing to invest hope and trust in himself, his fellows, and his world. To refrain, in the absence of preponderating reasons to the contrary, from letting hope influence belief—even to the mere extent of that sort of tentative belief at issue in a working assumption made for practical purposes—betokens a crabbed failure of confidence that has nothing admirable about it.

Accordingly, the failure to make a transition from axiological to doxastic theism, though certainly not manifesting any deficiency in logic, does betoken a somewhat regrettable failure of moral nerve. In the absence of a conviction that its realizability is infeasible, rational people seek to *implement* their desires in action—and one of the ways in which we can implement a desire is by letting it guide our beliefs, by letting the wish be father to the thought insofar as circumstances permit.

Be this as it may, the fact remains that an axiological approach to theism, while perhaps nonstandard and even unorthodox, is certainly not unprecedented. It reflects a recurrent leitmotif in Mediterranean monotheism. Its favorite Biblical text is the paradoxical "Lord, I believe; help thou mine unbelief." And there is no shortage of other passages in the Old and New Testaments alike on which such a position can draw for aid and comfort— texts that betray deep doubts about our ability to *know* God. As Job proclaims, "Oh that I knew where I might find him! that I might come even to his seat! . . . Behold I go forward, but he is not there; and backward, but I cannot perceive him." In the book of Psalms the stress is often not on what we know or believe of God, but on seeking, hoping, trusting. Merely to yearn for the Lord is, in the Psalmist's view, already to be well embarked on the road of faith. After all, a substantial part of the reason for the traditional Judeo-Christian emphasis on the mystery of God—as well as a substantial part of the message of religious mysticism—is to deemphasize the credal aspects of religion, which takes the doctrinal line of a subscription to propositions that is so appealing to the philosophical mind. The axiological rather than doxastic approach clearly reflects this ever-recurrent, though—given the great influence of theorizing philosophers on the theologians— never even remotely dominant tendency within the great monotheistic religions.

SIXTEEN

Rationality and Happiness

IS RATIONALITY a good thing? The question has a rhetorical
air about it. Rationality, after all, is a matter of the intelligent
pursuit of appropriate ends.[1] And this is by its very nature a
positive quality—a "perfection" in the philosophical terminology of an earlier day. Still, when everything is said and done,
the question remains: are rational people happier? Does this key
aspect of the human condition—the proper use of our intelligence—pay off for us in this regard? This theme harks back to
deliberations that the thinkers of ancient Greece posed in the
question, "Is the wise man also happy?," a problem to which
they dedicated much thought, concern, and controversy, and
which has every bit as much interest today as it did in the first
millennium B.C.

Two Modes of "Happiness"

As often happens with philosophical questions, the pivotal
issue is not simply one of examining facts, but predominantly
one of clarifying concepts and ideas. For the problem of the
linkage between rationality and happiness hinges critically on

[1] It is thus clear that rationality is here construed as involving more than a
capacity to move efficiently to *arbitrary* (and themselves unexamined) ends.
Someone who pursues (however effectively) an inherently absurd or inappropriate end is *not* being rational. Rationality overall involves both *inferential* rationality (valid reasoning) and *evaluative* rationality (appropriate appraisal).

just how we propose to understand the idea of "happiness."
A closer look at this conception is thus in order. Distinctions
must loom large here. In particular, we face two crucially diverse
alternatives, depending on whether we construe happiness in
an *affective* or in a *reflective* sense—whether we conceive of it
as a psychological state of subjective feeling and emotion or
as a judgmental matter of rational assessment and reflective
evaluation. This distinction between affective happiness and
reflective happiness stands as follows. Figuratively put, affective happiness depends on the viscera, and reflective happiness depends on the brain. The difference turns on whether
one responds to things positively by way of an emotive *psychological* reaction, some sort of warm inner affective glow, or
whether one responds to them by way of a rationalized pro-
appraisal, a deliberate intellectual *judgment* of the condition of
things.

As a psychological state, *affective* happiness is a matter of how
one *feels* about things—a matter of mood or sentiment. Primarily, it turns on what would commonly be called enjoyment
or pleasure. It is the sort of psychic state or condition that could,
in theory, be measured by an euphoriometer and represents the
sort of physiologically engendered condition that might be—
and indeed can be—induced by drugs or drink. (Think of the
"happy hour" at cocktail bars.)

By contrast, *reflective* happiness is a matter of how one *thinks*
about things. It is reflected in appraisal and judgment—in how
one assesses or evaluates the prevailing situation, rather than
how one reacts to it emotionally or affectively or physically. It is
not a psychological state of feeling at all, but an intellectual
stance of reflectively positive evaluation. It is a matter of being
so circumstanced as to appraise one's condition with warranted
judgmental approbation. The issue is one of rational satisfaction
rather than pleasure, of *eudaimonia* rather than *hēdonē*. Happiness in this second sense consists in the reflective contentment
of one who "*thinks* himself fortunate" for good and sufficient
reason. Its pivot is not *euphoria of feeling* but *contentment of mind*
on the basis of reflective appraisal.

The two sorts of "happiness" accordingly also have very different temporal aspects. Affective happiness (pleasure) is generally something fleeting and short-term—a thing of psychic

moods and whims, of the feeling of the moment. Reflective happiness (rational contentment) is generally something deeper and less transient—a matter of understanding rather than feeling, of stable structure rather than transitory state. Its crux is not just a matter of feeling satisfied with one's life but of being rationally entitled to be so.

Very distinct issues are accordingly at stake. People may well take reflective satisfaction (quite legitimately) in actions or occurrences that, like Kantian works of duty, do not at all promote their "happiness" in any affective sense of that term—indeed that may even impose a cost in this regard. It does not follow that the person who prospers in happiness or welfare is thereby superior in "quality of life." (We come back to the cutting edge of John Stuart Mill's obiter dictum, "Better to be Socrates dissatisfied than a pig satisfied.") And our attitude toward these matters tends to be very different. Toward people or nations that enjoy—even to abundance—the benefits of affective happiness, we may well feel a certain envy, but our admiration and *respect* could never be won on this basis. For these issues are judgmental and accordingly bear on reflective happiness alone.

Given these two very different ways of interpreting the idea of "happiness," it should be stressed that which of them one adopts will make all the difference for the question of how rationality and happiness are interrelated. On the one hand, if happiness is construed in the *reflective* sense as rational satisfaction, then the use of rationality is a promising way to increase one's happiness. For one thing, people who proceed rationally are, thanks to their rationality, going to improve the chances that things will eventuate favorably for the promotion of their real interests. And even when things do go wrong—as, life being what it is, they doubtless often will—the rational person has the consolation of rationality itself, of the recognition of having done his or her best. For the rational person prizes reason itself and takes rational satisfaction in the very fact of having done what reason demands. Even when matters go awry "due to circumstances beyond one's control," the rational agent has that contenting consolation of "having done one's best in the face of the inevitable" that was so greatly prized by the ancient Stoics. Realizing the limits of human powers—their own included— rational people avoid pointless regrets and futile recriminations, achieving the self-respect and justified self-satisfaction that goes with the realization that they have done all they can in a good cause. But the crux is this: reflective happiness pivots on the cultivation of our real or best interests—the realization of those conditions that are life-enhancing and best enable us to realize our opportunities for the attainment of genuine goods. And only reason can provide us with useful guidance about these matters. Deliberations of this sort combine to indicate that *if* happiness is construed in terms of one's reflective contentment with the condition of things by way of intellectual appraisal, *then* there is indeed good reason to think that the rational person will indeed fare better in the pursuit of happiness by virtue of that rationality.

On the other hand, if happiness is viewed as an *affective* psychic condition—a matter of accumulating points on the euphoriometer—then the thesis that rationality promotes happiness becomes very questionable. For one thing, there is the fact that we can gain ready access to euphoria through avenues not particularly endorsed by reason—through drugs and psychic manipulation, for example. For another, the very fact that we can speak of "harmless pleasures" indicates that there are also harmful ones, of which reason is bound to disapprove. By its very nature reason is geared not to our pleasure but to what is in our best interests, and so there is no basis for thinking that heeding reason's dictates will advantage us in the pursuit of affective pleasure.[2]

But surely rationality can help people to secure their objectives—to gain wealth, cultivate friends, influence people, and

[2] It is useful to observe the close parallelism of these ideas to discussions in the post-Aristotelian schools of Greek philosophy. The distinction between affective happiness and reflective happiness runs parallel to their distinction between pleasure or enjoyment (*hēdonē*) on the one hand and genuine well-being (*eudaimonia*) on the other. And if one identifies *rationality* with what those ancients called wisdom (*sophia*), then their insistence on wisdom as a necessary (though not necessarily sufficient) condition for the achievement of *true* happiness (well-being = *eudaimonia* = human flourishing) parallels our present conclusion that rationality is bound to facilitate reflective happiness. The discussions of those classical moralists are intimately relevant to our present deliberations, and point toward results of much the same general tendency. (Where wisdom rather than "know-how" is concerned, there is no technological obsolescence.) For an informative and interesting treatment of the relevant issues, see J. C. B. Gosling and C. C. W. Taylor, *The Greeks on Pleasure* (Oxford, 1982).

generally improve their chances of acquiring the good things of the world. On this basis, somebody is likely to object: "Surely rational people are the happier for their rationality, even in the affective mode of happiness, because their intelligence is capable of benefiting them in this regard as well." Now it would doubtless be very nice if this were so. But alas it is not. For while intelligence can lead one to water, it cannot ensure that drinking produces any worthwhile effects. There is no reason to think that conducting their affairs intelligently specifically benefits people in terms of increased affective happiness. Even getting more than one's share of the world's good things does not lead to this objective. There are simply too many other factors involved.

To be sure, there is the fact that rational people will be the more "knowledgeable"—that they will (presumably) transact their cognitive and their practical affairs with greater success in the realization of their objectives. But this will not mean all that much for their specially *hedonic* happiness. For experience teaches that people are not generally made affectively happier by "getting what they want." This, after all, very much depends on the kind of thing they are after. And even if people indeed are after the things of which reason approves, this will not help them all that much when affective or hedonic happiness is at issue. For affective happiness is too ephemeral and capricious to lend itself to effective manipulation by rational means. (Even—and perhaps especially—people who "have everything" may fail to be happy; there is nothing all that paradoxical or even unusual about someone who says, "I know that in these circumstances I *should* be happy, but I'm just not."[3]) Affective happiness largely is a matter of moods and frames of mind—easily frustrated by boredom or predictability. It is an ironic aspect of the human condition that affective happiness is inherently resistant to rational management.

Of course, people who proceed rationally will be disappointed less often than they otherwise would be. Their rationality can plausibly be expected to spare them sundry unpleasant surprises. But by the same token, rationality may also possibly

[3] Recall Edward Arlington Robinson's somber poem about Richard Corey, the man who "had everything to make us wish that we were in his place" and yet one night "went home and put a bullet through his head."

occasion its bearer some pain and dismay. For rational foresight and foreknowledge can also lead to painful apprehensions and gloomy forebodings about the likelihood of things going wrong—as they are bound to do in many instances. Rationality has far less bearing on affective happiness than we might ideally like.

Judge this from your own experience! Among the people you know, are the rational ones—the intelligent and sagacious and prudent ones—any happier, on balance, *affectively* speaking, than their more thoughtless and happy-go-lucky compatriots? Most likely not. On all indications, an easygoing disposition and a good sense of humor count far more with affective happiness than intelligence and rationality. No doubt, matters here will hinge less on "savvy" than on "luck"—on the disposition one has inherited and on whether one has the good fortune of living in times when things by and large go well—or at any rate improve on what has gone before.

To be sure, it might seem on first thought that the single-mindedly efficient pursuit of affective happiness is bound to provide greater pleasure in the long run. But the facts of experience teach otherwise. John Stuart Mill's description of his own experience is instructive in this regard. In a striking passage in his *Autobiography* he wrote:

It was in the autumn of 1826. I was in a dull state of nerves, such as everybody is occasionally liable to. . . . In this frame of mind, it occurred to me to put the question directly to myself: "Suppose that all your objects in life were realized; that all . . . could be completely effected at this very instant: would this be a great joy and happiness to you?" And an irrepressible self-consciousness distinctly answered, "No!" At this my heart sank within me: the whole foundation on which my life was constructed fell down.
. . .

The experiences of this period had two very marked effects on my opinions and character. In the first place, they led me to adopt a theory of life, very unlike that on which I had before acted, and having much in common with what at that time I certainly had never heard of, the anti-self-consciousness theory of Carlyle. I never, indeed, wavered in the conviction that happiness is the test of all rules of conduct, and the end of life. But I now thought that this end was only to be attained by not making it the direct end. Those only are happy (I thought) who have their minds fixed on some object other than their own happiness;

on the happiness of others, on the improvement of mankind, even on some art or pursuit, followed not as a means, but as itself an ideal end. Aiming thus at something else, they find happiness by the way. The enjoyments of life (such was now my theory) are sufficient to make it a pleasant thing, when they are taken *en passant*, without being made a principal object.[4]

Getting what we naïvely and unevaluatedly want can be a hollow business. And ironically, when hedonically affective happiness is *pursued*, however rationally and intelligently, it inclines to flee. (This is yet one more way in which the project of "the *pursuit* of happiness" faces substantial inherent difficulties.) For as Mill's ruminations indicate, rationality itself teaches us in the school of bitter experience about the ultimate emptiness of this sort of thing—its inherent incapacity to deliver on the crucial matter of real contentment by way of reflective happiness.

Considerations of this sort combine to indicate the implausibility of holding that rational people are the happier for their rationality, when happiness is construed in the hedonic terms of affective euphoria or pleasure.[5]

More on the Affective Rewards of Rationality

There is, however, a further importantly relevant aspect to the issue of rationality's bearing on happiness in its affective dimension. For our deliberations have to this point neglected an important distinction, in that the hedonic domain actually has two sides—the positive, which pivots on affective happiness or pleasure, and the negative, which pivots on affective unhappiness or pain.

A negatively oriented affective benefit is the removal or diminution of something bad. (It is illustrated in caricature by the story of the man who liked knocking his head against a wall because it felt so good when he stopped.) A positively oriented affective benefit, on the other hand, involves something that is

---

[4]*The Autobiography of John Stuart Mill*, ed. J. J. Coss (New York, 1929), pp. 94, 101.
[5]To be sure, the fact remains that rational people will certainly be better off (reflectively speaking) on rationality's account—seeing that they are bound to take satisfaction in rationality itself.

pleasant in its own right rather than by way of contrast with a distressing alternative.

This distinction bears importantly on our problem. For there is no doubt that the state of human well-being has been, and still can be, greatly improved through the use of intelligence in science and technology to secure the negatively oriented benefits of reduced human misery and suffering. Consider only a few instances: medicine (the prevention of childhood diseases through innoculation, anesthetics, plastic and restorative surgery, hygiene, dentistry); waste disposal and sanitation; temperature control (heating and air conditioning); transportation and communication; and so on. It would be easy to multiply examples of this sort many times over. Intelligence can certainly stand us in good stead in averting causes of distress and boredom. In decreasing such negativities, it can vastly improve the "quality of life" for people.

But the unfortunate fact remains that, as the world turns, this diminution of the negative does not necessarily yield positive repercussions for affective happiness. A decrease in suffering and discomfort does not produce a positive condition like pleasure or joy or happiness. For pleasure is not the mere absence of pain, nor joy the absence of sorrow. The removal of the affectively negative just does not of itself create a positive condition—though, to be sure, it abolishes an obstacle in the way of positivity. And so, the immense potential of modern science and technology for the alleviation of suffering and distress does not automatically qualify it as a fountain of affective happiness. The harsh fact of the matter is that technical rationality is usually ineffective as a promoter of ongoing hedonic happiness in its positive dimension.

To be sure, technical intelligence can indeed provide such enhancers of short-term affective positivity as alcoholic beverages or drugs. But there is a very big fly in this ointment. The affective pleasure of such euphoria inducers soon becomes eroded by routinization. Habituation swiftly undermines the pleasantness of these "pleasures." So that overall little if any real pleasure accrues from their merely nominal "enjoyment." In the end, it is not the pleasure of indulgence but the discomfort of deprivation that comes to prevail. Natural psychological and physical mechanisms soon transmute the "benefits" at issue with these technically contrived euphoria inducers from a positive to a negative character. The contribution of these technical resources, designed for the enhancement of pleasure, is soon reduced to the diminution of pain. No doubt rationality pays. But the irony of the human condition is that as far as *affective* matters are concerned, the utility of reason is vastly more efficacious in averting unhappiness than in promoting happiness in its positive dimension.

The Distrust of Reason

It is sometimes said that a person's rationality can actually impede the realization of happiness. After all, man does not live by reason alone, and many rewarding human activities—family life, social interaction, sports and recreations, "light" reading, films and other entertainment, and so on—make little or no use of reason or reasoning. And so, people often say things like: "Rationality as such is cold, passionless, inhumane. It stands in the way of those many life-enhancing, unreflective spontaneous activities that have an appropriate place in a full, rewarding, happy human life." One frequently hears such claims made. But they are profoundly mistaken.

Admittedly, there is more to humanity than rationality as such. Our natural makeup is complex and many-sided—a thing of many strains and aspects. We have interests over and above those at issue in the cultivation of reason. But there is no reason whatever why our reason should not be able to recognize this fact. To fail to do so would be simply unintelligent—and thus contrary to the very nature of rationality. The very fact that we are *animals* means that there is a good deal more to us than reason alone—and nothing prevents reason from recognizing that this is so. For reason can and does acknowledge as wholly proper and legitimate a whole host of useful activities in whose conduct it plays little if any part—socializing, diversions, recreations, and so on. Reason itself is perfectly willing and able to give them its stamp of approval, recognizing their value and usefulness.

People can certainly neglect those various valuable nonrational activities in favor of overcalculation, overplanning, and an inflated overcommitment to reasoning. However, the salient fact is that rationality itself recommends against this. In being "too rational" one would, strictly speaking, not be rational enough. It is perfectly rational sometimes to do heedless or even madcap things in this life—"to break the monotony" and inject an element of novelty and excitement into an otherwise prosaic existence. All work and no play makes life go stale. People can sometimes take quite appropriate pleasure from "irrational" actions—climbing mountains, betting on the ponies, riding the rapids of a rushing river. To break the mold of a colorless rationalism is, within limits, not all that irrational: it is part and parcel of a deeper rationality that goes beyond the superficial. After all, rationality aims at goods as well as goals. By its very nature, it is not stupid. It is clearly in a position to appreciate the value of enjoyment as well as that of achievement.

Accordingly, one really cannot be "too rational for one's own good." If, contrary to fact, there were such a defect—if this could be established at all—then reason itself could recognize and confront this circumstance. Intelligence does not stand as one limited faculty over against others (emotion, affection, and the like). It is an all-pervasive light that can shine through to every endeavor—even those in which reason itself is not involved. Reason itself is in the end our only trustworthy guide to whatever human undertakings are valid and appropriate. It is the exercise of rationality that informs us about priorities. For that very reason, reason itself takes top priority.

Several among the ancient philosophers—Aristotle preeminently—insisted on the primacy of the strictly intellectual pleasures inherent in the exercise of reason. They maintained that only the purely rational intellectual activities—learning, understanding, reasoning—yield satisfactions of a sort worthy of a rational being. Only in the pleasures of the mind did they see true satisfactions. Accordingly, they suggested that a truly rational being can take appropriate satisfaction only in the pleasures consequent on the exercise of reason—that all else is dross and delusion.

But this line of thinking is deeply problematic. Rationality does not require us to take satisfaction in reason alone and view the pleasures of reason as solely and uniquely genuine. Far from it! Reason can and does acknowledge the need for diversity and variation; it can and does recognize the importance of activities that make little or no call on its own resources. The importance of a *balance* of varied goods within a complex economy of values is something that reason itself emphasizes—even though this economy of values must itself encompass various mundanely nonrational goods. To insist that rational satisfaction—reflective contentment—rather than mere "pleasure" is the pivot of genuine happiness does not mean that commonplace pleasures have no legitimate place in a truly happy life. There is no sound reason why rational people need be spoilsports.

A deep distrust of reason is a leitmotiv of Spanish philosophy that runs from Francisco Sánchez and Gracián y Morales in the seventeenth century to Miguel de Unamuno and José Ortega y Gasset in the twentieth. What the Spaniards have against reason is that it is not an adequate basis for a satisfying life. As they see it, reason directs people to specifically "reasonable" and paternalistically "sensible" ends that can be objectively validated through the approval of others (experts). But the pursuit of such ends do not make people happy. "Be reasonable!" is the ever-repeated cry of disillusioned middle age against the sanguine enthusiasms of youth. And this eternal cry is destined to be eternally unavailing because youth realizes instinctively—and rightly—that the way to happiness does not lie in this particular direction.

This Spanish perspective combines a commonsensical view of the good life with a deep skepticism that *reason* can get us there. For the world—and in particular the social world in which we humans live—is changeable, chaotic, irrational. "General principles" are of little help; the useful lessons of life are those learned in the school of bitter experience. So urge the Spaniards.

All of this has a certain surface plausibility. But even in a difficult and disorderly world, people who do not examine it rationally—and refuse to profit from a reason-guided exploitation of the experience of others—certainly create needless difficulties for themselves. To be sure, there are other guides to human decision than reason itself—custom, instinct, experience, and spontaneous inclination among them. But only reasoned examination can teach us about their proper use and can inform us about the extent to which it makes sense to rely on them.

What is particularly ironic in the Spanish distrust of reason is its inevitable reliance on reason for validation. That reason may have its limits as a guide to the attainment of a satisfying life may well be true. But only reason itself can inform us about this—only rational scrutiny and a reason-guided contemplation about the matter can reliably inform us what these limits are. And so, in developing their case for the limitations of reason, the Spaniards are (inevitably) constrained to make use of the resources of reason. And this is exactly as it should be. Any *reasoned* critique of reason must rely on reason's own resources.

To be sure, various theorists mock reason as an exercise in futility. "Any defense of reason is predetermined to failure. For it must make use of the very instrument that is in question, and therefore commits the vicious circle fallacy." What nonsense! Whatever circularity is at issue is altogether virtuous. Reason is and *must* be self-endorsing. Self-validation is the only thing that makes sense here. The only defense of reason worth having is of course a rational one. What more—or what else—could a sensible person ask for?

Yet does rationality not undermine the emotional and affective side of human beings—the uncalculating, unselfish, open, easygoing, relaxed side that is no less significant in the overall scheme of human affairs than the sterner enterprise of "pursuing our ends"? Is reason not deficient in one-sidedly emphasizing the "calculating" aspect of human nature? Not at all! There are good grounds for reason *not* to deny the claims of our emotional and affective side. For life is infinitely fuller and richer that way! Reason, after all, is not our sole guide. Emotion, sentiment, and the affective side of our nature have a perfectly proper and highly important place in the human scheme of things—no less important than the active striving for ends and goals. Insofar as other valid human enterprises exist, there is good reason why reason can (and should) recognize and acknowledge them.

To say that reason is cold, inhumane, bloodless, and indifferent to human values is to misconceive it badly by misinterpreting it as purely a matter of means to arbitrary ends, committed to the approach of "let's get to the goal but never mind how, with no worry about who or what gets hurt along the way." Such an overnarrow, "mechanical" view of reason, regrettably widespread though it is, is totally inappropriate. It rests on the familiar fallacy of seeing reason as a limited-purpose instrument that is in no position to look critically at the goals toward whose realization it is employed. In taking this view, it refuses to grant reason that which is in fact its definitive characteristic—the use of intelligence.

There is little question that, as one recent author puts it, "one can do harm to important human values by overemphasizing the values of theorizing and cognition."[6] Yet acknowledging this nowise undermines the claims of reason. On the contrary! It is reason itself that demands that we recognize the limited place of the virtues of cognition, inquiry, and the cerebral side of life. An adequate account of rationality must rightly stress its importance and primacy while recognizing that the intellectual virtues are only limited components of the good life.

But is reason not defective because—as one hears it said—it generally counsels a prudent caution that is at odds with righteous indignation, courage, bravery, and other manifestations of the "spirited" side of human life? William Shakespeare's Troilus put this point as follows:

> You know a sword employed is perilous,
> And reason flies the object of all harm.
>   . . . Nay, if we talk of reason
> Let's shut our gates and sleep. Manhood and honor
> Should have hare-hearts, would they but fat their thoughts
> With this crammed reason. Reason and respect
> Make livers pale and lustihood deject.[7]

But here we have once more a too-narrow conception of reason. Reason is perfectly capable of acknowledging that "sweet reasonableness" is not called for everywhere and in all circumstances, recognizing (for example) that there may be occasion for indignation and outrage in a just cause.

What can and must be said on reason's behalf is that it is the very best guide we have for the management of our lives' doings and dealings. But it nevertheless remains an imperfect and never altogether satisfactory guide. For in this regard, those somber Spaniards are completely right. The role of chance and luck in human affairs means that our existence is always in large degree a riddle and a conundrum. In the end, problems of life have no straightforwardly rational solution because the management of a

---

[6] Stephen Nathanson, *The Ideal of Rationality* (Atlantic Highlands, N.J., 1985), p. 157. This book is well worth reading on the subject of our present concerns.
[7] *Troilus and Cressida*, II, ii, 40–41, 46–50.

satisfying life is no less a matter of the virtues of character than a matter of those of the intellect. And of course none of this comes as news to reason. As we have noted, it is of the essence of reason to insist on the intelligent cultivation of appropriate ends. And insofar as those various nonrational activities do indeed have value for us, reason itself is prepared to recognize and approve this. The life of reason is not wholly a thing of calculating, planning, striving. For us humans, rest, recreation, and enjoyment are very much a part of it. Accordingly, reason is perfectly willing to delegate a proper share of authority to our inclinations and psychological needs. It goes against reason to say that rational calculation should pervade all facets of human life. Reason does not insist on running the whole show, blind to its limitations in being simply one human resource among others. After all, rationality need not be unintelligent about it and overlook the importance for us of values outside the intellectual domain. What is counterproductive is not the reasonableness of rationality but the unreasonableness of an exaggerated rationalism.

In sum, it emerges that those who distrust reason do not properly understand what is at issue. By misidentifying true rationality with cold calculation, they do grave injustice to the nature of intelligence. People who think that rationality is at odds with happiness either have a distorted notion of rationality or have a distorted notion of happiness.

Reason as a Basis for Reflective Happiness

The upshot of these deliberations on how rationality bears on happiness is clear enough, even though subject to various complicating distinctions. If we construe happiness in the more reflective mode as an intellectual matter of rational contentment, then the rational person is bound to be the better off by way of improved chances for happiness. But if happiness is construed in the affective mode as a matter of pleasure or euphoria, then there are no good grounds for thinking that rationality is profitable for happiness in its positive aspect—though even here it does have the merit of being able to help in averting affective unhappiness. The outcome to the question of rationality's claims as a supporter of human happiness is accordingly indecisive. The answer will depend crucially on just which sort of conception of happiness we propose to adopt. We thus arrive at a result that is not perhaps all that surprising. Given that rationality is a matter of intelligence—of the effective use of mind—it is only natural and to be expected that rationality should be congenial to and supportive of that reflective, judgmental mode of happiness over which mind itself is the final arbiter.[8]

[8] Some of the material of this chapter is drawn from my book, *Rationality* (Oxford, 1988).

Index of Personal Names

Index of Personal Names

Library of Congress Cataloging-in-Publication Data

Rescher, Nicholas.
 Human interests : reflections on philosophical anthropology /
Nicholas Rescher.
  p.   cm.
 ISBN 0-8047-1811-3 (alk. paper) :
  1. Philosophical anthropology. 2. Man. I. Title.
 BD450. R444   1990   90-30349
 128—dc20   CIP

 ∞   This book is printed on acid-free paper